Cambridge Elements

Elements in Politics and Society in East Asia
edited by
Erin Aeran Chung
Johns Hopkins University
Mary Alice Haddad
Wesleyan University
Benjamin L. Read
University of California, Santa Cruz

AF588255

REFUGEE POLICIES IN EAST ASIA

Petrice R. Flowers
Center for Indo-Pacific Affairs and Matsunaga Institute for Peace and Conflict Resolution, University of Hawai'i at Mānoa

CAMBRIDGE
UNIVERSITY PRESS

Shaftesbury Road, Cambridge CB2 8EA, United Kingdom

One Liberty Plaza, 20th Floor, New York, NY 10006, USA

477 Williamstown Road, Port Melbourne, VIC 3207, Australia

314–321, 3rd Floor, Plot 3, Splendor Forum, Jasola District Centre, New Delhi – 110025, India

103 Penang Road, #05–06/07, Visioncrest Commercial, Singapore 238467

Cambridge University Press is part of Cambridge University Press & Assessment, a department of the University of Cambridge.

We share the University's mission to contribute to society through the pursuit of education, learning and research at the highest international levels of excellence.

www.cambridge.org
Information on this title: www.cambridge.org/9781009507288

DOI: 10.1017/9781108999427

© Petrice R. Flowers 2025

This publication is in copyright. Subject to statutory exception and to the provisions of relevant collective licensing agreements, no reproduction of any part may take place without the written permission of Cambridge University Press & Assessment.

When citing this work, please include a reference to the DOI 10.1017/9781108999427

First published 2025

A catalogue record for this publication is available from the British Library

ISBN 978-1-009-50728-8 Hardback
ISBN 978-1-108-99553-5 Paperback
ISSN 2632-7368 (online)
ISSN 2632-735X (print)

Cambridge University Press & Assessment has no responsibility for the persistence or accuracy of URLs for external or third-party internet websites referred to in this publication and does not guarantee that any content on such websites is, or will remain, accurate or appropriate.

Refugee Policies in East Asia

Elements in Politics and Society in East Asia

DOI: 10.1017/9781108999427
First published online: January 2025

Petrice R. Flowers
Center for Indo-Pacific Affairs and Matsunaga Institute for Peace and Conflict Resolution, University of Hawai'i at Mānoa

Author for correspondence: Petrice R. Flowers, pflowers@hawaii.edu

Abstract: East Asia stands apart from the rest of Asia in the prevalence of the institutionalization of the 1951 Refugee Convention. Despite this widespread adoption of the Convention in East Asia, the record on implementation into domestic law and policy is uneven. This Element offers a comparative analysis of the gap between the institutionalization of the Refugee Convention and the implementation of refugee policy in China, Japan, South Korea, Hong Kong, Taiwan, Macau, and Mongolia. Specific attention is given to two key policy issues: refugee status determination – deciding who is granted government recognition as a refugee – and complementary forms of protection – protection based on statutes other than the Refugee Convention. This Element demonstrates that implementation of the Refugee Convention in East Asia depends on a vibrant civil society with the space and opportunity to engage with local UNHCR offices, local branches of international nongovernmental organizations (INGOs), and other stake holders.

Keywords: refugee protection, implementation, refugee status determination, complementary protection, East Asia

© Petrice R. Flowers 2025

ISBNs: 9781009507288 (HB), 9781108995535 (PB), 9781108999427 (OC)
ISSNs: 2632-7368 (online), 2632-735X (print)

Contents

1 Introduction

In 2019, the United Nations High Commissioner for Refugees (UNHCR) identified 9.5 million people of concern in the Asia Pacific Region. Of those, 44 percent were refugees (4.2 million) and asylum seekers (212,000), people who have fled their homes and have a well-founded fear of being persecuted if they return to their country of origin. Indeed, Asia is the region that harbors the largest share of the world's refugees; it is also the region with the fewest governments that have ratified the 1951 International Convention for the Status of Refugees (hereafter, the Refugee Convention or the Convention). Whereas the multilateral treaty to protect refugees received broad support from Western countries, and the European Union, the Organization of African Unity, and Organzation of American States have since implemented regional agreements to strengthen refugee protection and address some of the Convention's shortcomings, fewer than half of states in Asia have ratified the Convention to date. This has become known as "Asian Rejection" of the Refugee Convention.

East Asian countries are the exception to "Asian Rejection" of the Refugee Convention. Although many Asian nations offered at least temporary protection for refugees fleeing Vietnam, Cambodia, and Laos in the 1970s, China, Japan, and South Korea institutionalized the Convention through ratification between 1981 and 1992. In practice, the absence of policies to implement the Convention meant that there was little difference between these countries and the rest of Asia in their lack of commitment to protect refugees. However, this changed in the early 2000s, when more support for refugee protection developed in East Asia's civil societies, and East Asian governments began implementing domestic policies to protect refugees. The Japanese government, for example, made a series of revisions to its Immigration Control and Refugee Recognition Act. In 2010, it became the first Asian nation to establish a refugee resettlement program to work in conjunction with the United Nations. In 2005, Taiwan proposed a Refugee Act, although it still has not passed the legislature. South Korea established refugees' right to work and enacted a comprehensive Refugee Protection Act in 2012; the Act went into effect in 2013. South Korea's Refugee Act allowed for resettlement of refugees in the country, and to that end, a pilot resettlement program ran from 2015 to 2017; this program made South Korea the second Asian nation to establish a refugee resettlement program. In 2014, Hong Kong established a Unified Screening Mechanism to evaluate claims of *non-refoulement*, the most basic right that refugees can claim to protect them from being returned to a country where they have a well-founded fear of persecution. Mongolia's 1992 constitution is notable because it codifies the possibility of granting asylum in the country's highest law; a 2010 law reinforces access to asylum on grounds of political persecution. In 2012, China revised its Exit and Entry Administration Law outlining the criteria for asylum seekers to achieve legal recognition,

This Element examines the institutionalization and implementation of the Refugee Convention in East Asia, focusing on the latter. Institutionalization refers to the diffusion process across states at the international level; implementation is a parallel process at the domestic level. Ratification of international agreements is a central aspect of the process of institutionalization; however, these two terms are not interchangeable. The process of institutionalization includes negotiations that lead to signing and then ratifying the agreement. Institutionalization is progressive in that the process continues even after treaty ratification via periodic reviews of the progress of state parties, making them accountable to the international community. Implementation, by contrast, is about enacting the Convention domestically; usually, by passing laws to codify the norms and rules.

Given the significant temporal lag between institutionalization and implementation, if the analysis focused exclusively on explaining why many East Asian states institutionalized the Convention, we would miss the central puzzle of this study: the significant variation of implementation among East Asian jurisdictions. Robust refugee protection is about offering refugees the same economic, political, and social rights and protections as those afforded to citizens. Economic rights include the right to work and earn a living; political rights include legal status, a right to settle locally, access to naturalization processes, and freedom of movement. Social rights include the right to access social benefits such as housing, health care, schooling, et cetera. Granting recognition that acknowledges legal status allowing a refugee to remain and to work is the most basic level of implementation. Before Japan ratified the Convention, the Diet, its legislature, changed the national pension and health insurance laws to abolish the citizenship requirement. Both Japan and Korea revised their Immigration Control Acts to include refugee recognition so that these became Immigration Control and Refugee Recognition Acts; continued to make more changes over time. Korea and Macau have the most robust implementation. Korea now has a comprehensive law, the Refugee Act passed in 2012 that addresses the political, economic, and social rights of refugees as well as clearly codifying procedures for granting complementary protection (discussed below). Macau has laws that extend the same rights as citizens to recognized refugees. China has criteria for granting refugee recognition but they do not have clear, codified refugee status determination procedures necessary to grant legal status (discussed below). Taiwan and Mongolia do not have any laws implementing the Convention (Mongolia's law allowing protection based on political persecution is much narrower than the Convention). Hong Kong has a Unified Status Mechanism that protects refugees from *refoulement*, but they do not allow refugee resettlement so there are no laws implementing the Convention by extending economic, political, or social rights.

Studies of "Asian Rejection," a term used to describe Asia's resistance to the UN's leadership on refugee protection, offer a state-centric analysis that highlights the Refugee Convention's shortcomings and individual countries' leadership and top-down policy-making. I challenge this argument's relevance for contemporary East Asia. This explanation may have applied to East Asia in the post-WWII period through the 1960s when these countries were still recovering from the war and developing their economies. Now, nearly all the nations in East Asia have not only institutionalized the Refugee Convention but also many have taken significant steps at implementation.[1] In China's two Special Administrative Regions, Hong Kong and Macau, and self-governing Taiwan, claimed by Beijing and not recognized by the United Nations, actors on the ground are leveraging international norms and facilitating the implementation of refugee protection. East Asian acceptance of refugee protection began with the ratification of the Refugee Convention. That marked the start of a process that has extended to include domestic legislation and the creative use of complementary forms of protection, especially in areas where governments cannot ratify the Refugee Convention.

What has worked to improve refugee protection in East Asia has not been top-down policy so much as policy grounded in global-local connections, including networks of activists and NGOs. As we will see below, Japan's successive revisions to the Immigration Control and Refugee Recognition Act and South Korea's Refugee Act, for example, were the result of civil society organizations advocating for changes in existing policies. Although it has not yet born fruit, civil society organizations in Taiwan have publicized the existence of refugees in Taiwan and taken up the issue of passing protection legislation. Legislation has been proposed but has not yet passed. In Hong Kong, lawyers have successfully used the law to protect refugees from refoulement.

[1] The Democratic People's Republic of Korea (North Korea), Mongolia, and Taiwan are not parties to the Refugee Convention. Taiwan is not a party to any UN agreements because it is not allowed membership in the organization. When the UN recognized the Republic of China (Taiwan), it ratified the International Covenant on Civil and Political Rights, which includes a prohibition on refoulement. After the People's Republic of China (China) became officially recognized by the UN in 1972, Taiwan continued to adopt UN agreements and implement them into its laws. Despite the UN not recognizing Taiwan's assent, the island nation does institutionalize international agreements and implement them domestically. It has not done so in the case of the Refugee Convention.

This Element argues that the local context, specifically pressure from civil society, accounts for variations in Refugee Convention implementation across states. More specifically, this research finds that open societies with democratic political cultures, mature and robust civic organizations, and dense networks with government and NGOs are more likely to respond to pressure from below, build relationships, and establish networks essential for norm diffusion. Democratic political cultures mean activists and their organizations do not have to worry as much about negative blowback from their activities; NGOs have the political space and the will to push the government when necessary. Robust civil societies have a diversity of actors and organizations, which expands their influence. A robust civil society that is comprised of NGOs, epistemic communities, activists, and advocates is necessary for implementation. Their ability to leverage diverse actors increases the possibility that they can reach and influence policymakers and other powerful actors. A mature civil society engages with the government to advocate for policies that implement international norms domestically and can withstand the inevitable setbacks in refugee advocacy. Long-standing organizations are used to playing the long game; part of their expertise is born of a history of experience with actors and institutions. Mature civic organizations have been around long enough to have learned to accept partial victories when there is nothing more to gain; they will survive for the next fight.

When norms are diffused throughout an open society with a mature and robust civil society, there is more support for implementation and more resources that activists can draw from when government efforts at implementation fall short. Activists use dense connections developed over time to facilitate norm diffusion and support for implementation. Because implementation is ongoing, activists push the government to reform and refine policies long after adoption. The temporal gap between institutionalization and implementation allows for and requires broader and deeper norm diffusion throughout society to build public support for implementation. Recent scholarship on the Refugee Convention and refugee protection in Asia develops important arguments about contemporary bottom-up approaches to implementing norms of protection and completely bypassing institutionalization of the Refugee Convention. Nah (2016) shows how the creation of the regional NGO network the Asia Pacific Refugee Rights Network (APRRN), in 2008, ushered in new opportunities for domestic civil society organizations from across the Asia Pacific region. Perhaps most important was the space the network provided to develop a community of practice that strengthened the visibility, capacity, and connectedness of local civil society organizations, reconfiguring the power relations between them and powerful stakeholders such as the UNHCR and states, and the connections facilitated by APRRN helps local civil society organizations develop a regional imagination and engage in advocacy at the local, national, and international levels, increasing global-local connections around refugee issues.

Choi (2019) builds on this by specifying how bottom-up approaches to refugee protection were manifested in practices that grew out of the APPRN regional network space. His analysis of the APRRN shows how this network played a key role in reconfiguring the approach to refugee protection in the region from one based on seeking to convince states to institutionalize the Refugee Convention to one that focused on implementation from below – with or without institutionalization. Choi argues that practices, principles, and policies to implement refugee protection are based on APRRN's "interpretation of human rights laws and norms that introduces alternative frameworks, mobilizes material and non-material resources and shares information" (Choi 2019, 170). The alternative frameworks focus on national-level legal protections instead of institutionalizing the Refugee Convention. APRRN and its various working groups engage in refugee advocacy at the national level and in sharing best practices to help members build their capacity. For example, in 2016 the Legal Aid and Advocacy working group tried to replicate in Taiwan the success that a national network of Korean NGOs, including many APRRN members, had in initiating the legislation and eventually became South Korea's Refugee Act. Despite the failure of legislative efforts in Taiwan, Taiwanese civil society organizations were able to publicize the need for refugee protection in Taiwan to domestic and international audiences. In these and other cases, civil society in Asia sought to shift from a framework of understanding refugees as security threats to people deserving of human rights protections. Resource mobilization supported civil society's ability to engage with stakeholders nationally and internationally; perhaps most important was the ability for small NGOs to attend and participate in the global decision-making at the United National High Commissioner for Refugees (UNHCR) NGO Consultations in Geneva.

There are three main diffusion processes outlined in Section 3 below – localization, vernacularization, and global-local feedback loop – each with varying emphasis on the role of domestic nonstate actors. All of the cases examined here show that implementation is a politically contested, nonlinear process where domestic nonstate actors leverage the state's institutionalization of the Refugee Convention and/or the norm of protection embedded in the Convention to push for more and deeper implementation. Any particular policy outcome represents negotiated compromises that continue to evolve. Thus, understanding *process* is just as important as any one outcome.

In examining the implementation of the Refugee Convention, we will address how new support for refugee protection developed in East Asia – the People's Republic of China (China), Hong Kong SAR (Hong Kong), Macau SAR (Macau), the Republic of China (Taiwan), the Republic of Korea (South Korea), Japan, and Mongolia. Nonstate actors are at the core of implementing refugee protection in many East Asian nations. In states with vibrant civil societies, activists create conditions for implementation. Civil society actors and lawyers formed alliances in states that ratified the Convention, using human rights and their state's obligations under the Convention to frame their demands for refugee protection. States without robust civil societies have been least successful in implementing the Convention meaningfully.

Offering a comparative analysis of refugee policies in East Asia, I draw on field research conducted in Taiwan (2012), Japan (2003, 2009), and South Korea (2010) and on secondary literature to examine the evolution of relevant political landscapes from the late 1970s – when refugee protection began to affect the region directly – through 2019. My contemporary analysis concentrates on 2001–2019, the period when increased support for protecting refugees resulted in significant policy changes. I argue that global-local connections between domestic supporters of refugee protection and international norms and institutions tipped the balance in favor of refugee protection.

The case of refugee protection in East Asia highlights the power of global and local connections in norm diffusion to bring about change where more top-down efforts have failed. Section 2 will analyze data on the numbers of asylum applications, recognized refugees, and rejected applications in East Asia since 2001 to show how these countries differed little from others that had not adopted the Convention. Section three will focus on norm diffusion and implementation of the Convention. Sections 4 and 5 examine two specific issues around basic refugee protection – refugee status determination procedures (RSD) and complementary protection. These sections situate East Asia into broader theoretical debates in refugee studies and provide comparative analysis of empirical policies that are the two primary ways that refugees receive legal protection in East Asia. I will show that implementation depends on the local context, especially a vibrant civil society with the space to engage other stakeholders including local UNHCR offices, and local branches of international nongovernmental organizations (INGOs), such as Amnesty International.

1.1 Asian Rejection

The Refugee Convention is the centerpiece of the international refugee regime. Despite the large number of refugees in Asia, few states have adopted the

Convention. As of this writing, three of eleven Southeast Asian states have institutionalized the Convention: the Philippines, Cambodia, and, more recently, Timor-Leste (2003). In South Asia, only one of the eight states – Afghanistan (2005) – is a party to the Convention. Sara Davies' research is essential for understanding the history of the Refugee Convention in Asia from its early conception. In her 2006 analysis, Davies attempts to address the issue in the broader Asian region – including East Asia, South Asia, and Southeast Asia – which she defines as the 30 states UNHCR identifies as belonging to the Asian region. She critiques as inadequate three common explanations in the scholarly literature for why the region with one of the highest numbers of refugees has such a low Convention ratification rate: that reluctance stems from "good neighborliness" or a principle of noninterference in other countries' affairs, that "economic costs" to governments are too great, and that migrants, including refugees, contribute to "social disruption." All three of these arguments are rooted in colonial legacies in the region: dividing territory, imposing boundaries, and tying together state territory and nationality, population migration, and ethnic hierarchies.

Good neighborliness, a norm throughout Asia and a foundational norm of the Association of Southeast Asian Nations (ASEAN), is rooted in the norm of nonintervention in the affairs of sovereign states. Nonintervention is one of the core norms of the United Nations and the post-WWII international system. It is meant to deter aggression, protect territorial integrity, eliminate war, and strive for peace between members (Franck and Rodley 1973). In Asia, nonintervention became closely tied to the argument that Asian values required a "culturally and developmentally specific interpretation of rights" based on values shared throughout the region (Kingsbury and Avonius 2008).

The Cold War saw the development of the first stage of the Asian values debate, where attention was more focused on anti-colonial struggle and decolonization than on human rights. The second stage of the debate stretched from the end of the Cold War until the Asian financial crisis in the late 1990s. During this period, postcolonial countries focused on arguing that Asian culture offered an alternative to Western values of human rights and democracy. The most prominent voices in this alternative vision of modernity were Singapore's Lee Kuan Yew and Malaysia's Mahathir Mohammad. During this period, the nature of conflict had changed, and there was more international attention to human rights accompanied by increased pressure on repressive regimes in Asia to reform. In response, the Bangkok Declaration of 1993 exhibited a clear regional consensus that human rights, especially civil and political rights, were culturally specific and had to be understood within state contexts. This was essentially an argument against the universality of human rights. As East

Asian developmental states, the "Asian Tiger" economies became more ambivalent about human rights, ASEAN broadened the norm of nonintervention to include not meddling in or criticizing the domestic affairs of neighboring states – good neighborliness. Good neighborliness includes not criticizing other ASEAN members for human rights abuses, such as the treatment of minorities within their borders, which could escalate into the cause of outward migration and refugee flows (Muntarbhorn 1992). Asian values and good neighborliness continued to prioritize economic growth over human rights.

The developing economies concentrated in Southeast Asia – many received development aid from the United States (Acharya 2004) – argued that they could not afford to provide refugees with social welfare support, including education and healthcare, required under the Refugee Convention. They argued that already stretched budgets could not adequately provide services to their populations, so admitting refugees would add a burden they were not in a position to bear. Southeast Asian states argued that they could not afford to host refugees despite economically poorer states opening their doors to refugees (Suhrke 1993, 192). The history of colonialism and newly independent states in the region is one where there was significant overlap between domestic economic issues and ethnic identity, so these two issues are closely connected, and upsetting either can pose grave threats to state stability. Suhrke argues that ASEAN's strong rejectionism, which members insisted was based on economic concerns, is better explained by a political calculus that receiving states such as Malaysia made regarding challenges that outsiders would pose to ethnic balance and, therefore, social cohesion (Suhrke 1993).

When they gained independence, states such as Malaysia achieved internal peace and social cohesion by establishing delicate ethnic balances. Many of these states were especially sensitive to ethnic Chinese refugees because of the history of tensions between local ethnic populations and upwardly mobile Chinese migrants who settled throughout the region and became powerful actors in the economic landscape, often serving as middlemen between colonial settlers and native populations. In the case of Malaysia, the Muslim Malay-dominated government accepted a limited number of Muslim refugees from Cambodia and Burma but refused to accept any of the ethnic Chinese that largely made up the first and largest waves of refugees from Vietnam (Muntarbhorn 1992; Suhrke 1993). This ethnic affiliation is the same reason why China accepted and resettled more than 150,000 refugees from Vietnam while they have not accepted ethnic Kokangs and others fleeing Burma to resettle as refugees (Ibsen 2014; Choi 2017; Song 2017). Even Singapore, with its majority ethnic Chinese population, supported the strong rejectionism of the region. In this case, as the state with the largest ethnic Chinese population outside of China, Singapore had an interest in not becoming the default destination for ethnic Chinese who periodically face targeted violence and expulsion in the region.

In some countries, such as Japan, concerns about social cohesion do not focus on one specific ethnic group but on outsiders in general. One manifestation of this was that Japan's refugee policy is part of, not separate from, its immigration policy – a characteristic of refugee policies in all East Asian states that have adopted the Convention. The government amended the Immigration Control Act when Japan adopted the Refugee Convention and it became the Immigration Control and Refugee Recognition Act; South Korea undertook similar revisions to its immigration laws when it adopted the Convention. Approaching refugees as a migration issue instead of a human rights issue is a manifestation of the belief throughout Asia that refugees are really economic migrants; tying immigration and refugee policies together creates the migration-asylum nexus, discussed below. In multi-ethnic states such as Malaysia, which continues to reject the Refugee Convention, and states such as Japan, which eventually institutionalized the Convention but whose implementation policies continue to reflect the suspicion of all outsiders, there remains some flexibility in practice depending on shifting political calculations.

Davies (2008) argues that the Eurocentric process of writing the Convention marginalized Asian countries and their interests. The dominance of the United States and Europe in writing the Convention created a document that served their interests; thus, the gap between institutionalization and implementation has not been an issue. Later, when Southeast Asia experienced waves of refugee movements, beginning with the Indochinese refugee crisis after the United States left Vietnam, countries in the region that were not parties to the Refugee Convention could receive incentives from UNHCR and Western countries for protecting refugees. Indeed, it was exactly because these countries had no obligation to assist refugees crossing their borders that countries such as the United States stepped in with offers of financial assistance and refugee resettlement. Given that there was a benefit to the states in the region who were not party to the Convention in part because they had no obligation under the agreement, there remained no incentive to adopt the Convention later (Davies 2006, 2008).

The arguments explaining Asian Rejection of the Refugee Convention outlined above focus on the importance of material concerns such as economic resources and local ideational concerns rooted in cultural values. Such concerns are present across Asia. Understanding institutionalization and implementation of international agreements, such as the Refugee Convention, requires attention to both international and domestic processes. I have argued elsewhere that

Japan's state and national identity were two conflicting impulses that affected adopting and implementing the Refugee Convention (Flowers 2006). National identity based on a narrow conceptualization of "the Japanese" as a homogeneous nation manifests in immigration restrictions and discrimination against non-Japanese. National identity limits domestic implementation of the Refugee Convention as it requires the admission and incorporation of non-Japanese into Japanese society (Flowers 2006).

By contrast, Japan's state identity, based primarily on its status as an advanced economy and democracy, ties it very closely to the international community. Japan's status as an economic power comes with specific international obligations that have increased over time with the country's increasing wealth. Its status as a democracy shapes how these obligations are fulfilled (Flowers 2006). Subsequent research explored how international and domestic political practices interact and under what conditions international norms and law can contribute to domestic policy change. Analysis of three variables – state desire for legitimacy, strength of domestic advocates, and the degree of conflict between international and domestic norms – on the process of adopting the Refugee Convention shows that although there was a high degree of conflict between international and domestic norms on this issue, the state desire for legitimacy trumped that internal conflict and Japan adopted the Refugee Convention in 1981 (Flowers 2009, 2016). Analysis of Diet records reveals that government actors believed that if they reshaped Japan's identity into one more appropriate for a world economic power and developed country, international legitimacy would follow (Flowers 2009, chapter 3). These analyses and findings offer useful insights into the actions of other East Asian states.

1.2 East Asian Acceptance

There remains the question of why those few Asian nations that have adopted the Refugee Convention have done so and to what effect. Most Asian nations that have ratified the Convention – or territories in Asia where the Convention has been otherwise institutionalized – are in East Asia. Theories of international norm diffusion best explain why East Asian nations with different political systems have institutionalized the Refugee Convention. International norms scholars have established that state interests and identities are mutually constituted. States that identify as democracies or market economies share interests with other democratic states or market economies. Such interests are many and reflect community values. In the case of democracies, these values include respect for human rights, the rule of law, freedom of thought, et cetera. In the case of market economies these include pursuit of strong economies with a focus on economic growth. These interests and identities lead states to adopt international norms that establish standards of appropriate behavior (Klotz 1995; March and Olsen 1998; Reus-Smit 2017). I argue that democratization and marketization in states of the region (state identity) reconstituted state interests (as modern and/or democratic states) and led these states to institutionalize the Refugee Convention. Most studies that address the institutionalization of the Refugee Convention in East Asia offer (or take for granted) instrumental explanations of why individual East Asian states have adopted the Convention. These accounts outline a region where each state – China, Japan, and South Korea – acted independently to adopt the Refugee Convention without coordination or shared interests.

Traditionally, scholars understood Japan's international relations as rationalist responses to foreign pressure, *gaiatsu*. In the first book focused solely on Japan's refugee policy, Mukae (2001) argues that Japan's adoption of the Convention was a defensive action of a reactive state responding to foreign pressure. Adopting the Convention was possible because of the convergence of government interest to respond to foreign pressure and domestic supporters of the international refugee regime, who at the time consisted of elites such as Sadako Ogata, the longest-serving UN High Commissioner for Refugees. Japan adopted the Refugee Convention more than twenty-five years after joining the United Nations during the six years between 1979 and 1985 when it acceded to four core international human rights treaties – the International Covenant on Civil and Political Rights, the International Covenant on Economic, Social, and Cultural Rights, the Convention on the Elimination of All Forms of Discrimination Against Women, and the Refugee Convention. Adopting these treaties was Japan's attempt to get on board with the growing importance of human rights in global politics (Mukae 2001). Early studies critique Japan's failure to implement the rights and protections of the Refugee Convention into Japan's domestic law as an institutional failure (Mukae 2001; Akashi 2006; Arakaki 2007). Japan continued to have a poor record of protecting human rights, especially the human rights of foreigners. These and other rationalist explanations for Japan's acceptance of international agreements do shed light on the role of outside pressure in Japan ratifying the Convention. However, because other states react differently to outside pressure, these explanations do not help us understand the other East Asian cases.

The normative turn in the study of international relations that began in the late 1990s offered new theoretical frameworks for understanding world politics. Two innovations from this literature, attention to the role of the mutually constituted relationship between state interests and identity in world politics and the relationship between states' international and domestic politics, led to new insights on Japan's institutionalization of the Refugee Convention and implementation of refugee policy domestically. These innovations ushered in a new line of research that sought to situate Japan in an international context (Flowers 2006, 2008, 2009, 2010). Flowers (2006) argues that Japan's historically constituted and discursively constructed state identity accounts for the adoption of the Refugee Convention, and its national identity that conceptualizes "the Japanese" nation as monoethnic has been a limitation on compliance with the Convention. This study challenges the rationalist understanding of foreign pressure, *gaiatsu*, as materially based. Flowers shows how and why identity-based pressure affected Japan's adoption of the Refugee Convention. Flowers (2008) explores the role of nonstate actors in Japan's implementation of the Refugee Convention and argues that the lack of access to domestic political institutions, specifically the Ministry of Justice, and ideational constraints have hindered efforts by nonstate actors in Japan to reform refugee policies and bring them more in line with the Convention. Increasing attention to the role of nonstate actors and transnational relations has added depth to our understanding of how refugee protection norms diffused into Japan (Arakaki 2007; Dean and Nagashima 2007; Flowers 2010).

China adopted the Refugee Convention in 1981. In the most comprehensive study on refugee policy in China and its two special administrative regions, Song (2020a) situates China's adoption of the Convention into the reform and opening policies instituted in 1978–1979, followed by adoption of eight international human rights agreements from 1981 to 1984. She attributes China's accession to the Convention, at least partly, to a "desire to integrate into the international community" (Song 2020a, 24). China's refugee policies remain the least developed of the East Asian jurisdictions that have institutionalized the Convention. However, the government still has to contend with refugees who arrive in China due to conditions in the neighboring states of Vietnam, Burma/Myanmar, and North Korea. Ibsen (2014), Choi (2017), and Song (2017) offer comparative analyses to try to understand China's differential treatment of refugees depending on their origin. These three studies find that ethnicity matters in the government's willingness to accept groups as refugees and resettle them in China, findings that confirm the conclusions of earlier research discussed above (e.g., Muntarbhorn 1992; Suhrke 1993). Ethnic Kokangs and Kachins from Myanmar are not resettled or integrated to the extent that Vietnamese-born ethnic Chinese have been, but they have been allowed to stay in China as "border residents" (Song 2017). North Koreans have received the harshest treatment as they are designated illegal migrants who risk deportation to North Korea (Park 2011; Song 2018). Other studies do not focus on

China's refugee policy per se but make the case that the state should protect North Korean escapees as refugees under international refugee law (Chan and Schloehardt 2007; Kim 2012; Goedde 2011).

To understand East Asian institutionalization of the Refugee Convention, we must situate these states and their concerns into an analysis framed by the broader international context characterized by rapid economic growth and emerging democratic governments. Recent theorizing of norm diffusion among states and from international to domestic contexts helps us understand why East Asian states stand apart in Asia as having institutionalized the Refugee Convention and how implementation is proceeding unevenly across the region. International norms and state identity are mutually constituted. International norms, including those codified in international agreements like the Refugee Convention, set standards of appropriate behavior and govern membership and status in the international community. Which states institutionalize which norms depend partly on community membership or membership aspirations (e.g. Checkel 1997, Gurowitz 1999). International norms both draw on and establish hierarchical social order among states; policy advocates draw on these hierarchies to frame policy demands as appropriate and perhaps even expected behavior for a state, given its rank in a given international hierarchy of states (Towns 2012). For their part, states institutionalize international norms and policies to affirm their identity within a particular community of states and their rank in the international social hierarchy. In contemporary global politics, high status is accorded to those states that are modern and democratic. Flowers' (2009) findings that Japan adopted the Refugee Convention as a way of gaining international legitimacy resonates with Towns' theorizing on international norm diffusion and social rank. The broader framework of international norm diffusion and social hierarchy explains why East Asian nations, characterized by different regime types, adopted the Refugee Convention.

Human rights and refugee protection both emerged as central international concerns after WWII. Their status was highlighted and politicized when the United States made each an important part of the ideological war between the United States and the former Soviet Union and their respective allies. Human rights norms are both regulative and constitutive; they regulate state behavior by setting a standard of appropriate behavior, and they constitute certain kinds of states. Respect for human rights became one of the fundamental values of Western democracies, along with economic freedom (a market economy) and freedom of thought. Adoption of international human rights agreements has been an important way for states to demonstrate that they belong to the community of modern and/or democratic states. Mukae (2001), Arakaki

(2007), and Flowers (2009, 2016) support the argument that Japan adopted the core international human rights treaties to demonstrate its membership in the club of liberal democracies.

During the Cold War era, "refugees" became synonymous with dissidents fleeing the former Soviet Union, Eastern Bloc, and other communist countries. The United States saw refugees from communist countries as an indictment of communism and a confirmation of the moral superiority of democracy. As a result, the US government accepted large numbers of people who were assumed to be fleeing based on a well-founded fear of persecution based on their political beliefs (Goodwin-Gil 2008). China's adoption of both market reforms and the Refugee Convention challenged the narrative of these as characteristics that distinguished communist and democratic governments, as it was the first communist country to adopt this important human rights agreement.

Adopting the Refugee Convention in 1981, Japan affirmed its identity as an international economic power and democratic state. Institutionalizing the Refugee Convention in 1982 contributed to China's efforts to establish its identity as a modern state defined by a market economy, a project led by Deng Xiaoping's market reforms. When the South Korean government adopted the Convention in 1992 (Lee 2014), it established itself as a member of the community of democracies soon after its democratic consolidation with the 1987 election. The country further burnished its human rights credentials with the establishment of its National Human Rights Commission in 2001. The historical context during the period when Japan, South Korea, and China institutionalized the Refugee Convention supports the argument that concern about their position in the international social hierarchy accounts for institutionalization. For Japan and South Korea, the primary concern was their democratic credentials; for China, it was its economic credentials. In sum, for China, Japan and South Korea state interests, not the desire to protect refugees was the motivating factor for ratifying the Convention.

International hierarchies, such as those related to the history of colonization and empire in East Asia, have been central in shaping the region's migration patterns, including the movement of refugees (Morris-Suzuki 2010). The legacy of empire is also evident in Hong Kong and Macau: the systems for dealing with refugees in both of these "special administrative regions" are the direct result of their status until the late twentieth century as British and Portuguese colonies, respectively. In Taiwan, international politics of a different sort bars participation in the international refugee regime altogether. Mongolia is a former Soviet-influenced state that is now a democracy in a complicated geopolitical region.

2 Asylum Applications, Recognized Refugees, and Sending and Receiving in East Asia

Throughout Asia, refugees are often viewed as economic migrants whose primary motivation for moving is to improve the material conditions of their lives; they are often not seen as refugees with a well-founded fear of persecution upon returning to their country of origin. The perception that people claiming to be refugees are actually economic migrants bolsters arguments that refugees threaten social cohesion. Such arguments result in the securitization of refugees, whereby those seeking protection go from general threats to social cohesion to specific threats to national security. Kim's (2012) examination of South Korea's refugee policy significantly challenges the idea of migrants/refugees as threats. Kim investigates the migration-asylum nexus, critiquing how the unity of immigration and refugee policy in South Korea contributes to the discursive construction of migrant/refugee as a threat. To challenge the idea of refugees as threats, Kim argues that the migration-asylum nexus, where there is a constant shifting of identity between "migrant" and "refugee" in Asia, is partly due to the government's insistence on distinguishing between economic migrants and political refugees. This often-impossible task leads to refugee status determination procedures dragging on for years, further forcing refugees to become economic migrants as they live what Kim calls a "life on probation." In addition to novel theoretical insights, Kim also offers an empirically rich study that uses extensive fieldwork to build a thick description of how Burmese refugees in South Korea use participation in a transnational political community to improve their chances of gaining refugee status in South Korea. Schatte and McCann (2014) document a welcome shift in South Korea's approach to refugees from the emphasis on securitization rooted in the "illusion of an ethnically and culturally homogeneous population" toward greater alignment with international human rights norms and a focus on protection (Schatte and McCann 2014, 319). This study resonates with Flowers' (2009, 2016) attention to how domestic advocates leverage international human rights law to advocate for refugees. Since South Korea's Refugee Act was enacted in 2013, more recent scholarship centers on analysis and critique of the Act (e.g., Wolman 2013). These studies celebrate the significant achievement of the Refugee Act while highlighting its weaknesses. Like much of the research on refugee policy in East Asia, this scholarship uses theoretical insights rooted in rich empirical studies to produce policy-relevant work that urges more nuanced place-based understandings of refugee policy in East Asia that also have relevance beyond state borders.

Against this backdrop, this section will consider data on the number of asylum applications, recognized refugees, and rejected applications. These data are meant to provide a broad overview of how East Asian jurisdictions compare on these measures. These data help us understand the numbers of asylum seekers arriving in East Asia, how the numbers change over time, how jurisdictions compare with each other, and where refugees originate. We can see that significant numbers of asylum seekers did not begin arriving in East Asia until well after the Refugee Convention had been institutionalized in Japan, China, Taiwan, and Macau, suggesting that Convention ratification alone is not a significant "pull factor" as some states might fear. Even as the numbers of asylum seekers in East Asia have increased, these data demonstrate decisions granting refugee status in the region as a whole have not changed significantly between 2001 and 2019. So, even well after Convention ratification, East Asia did not offer significantly more protection than South East Asian states that rejected the Convention. The national-level data allows us to see trends and to interpret them in light of policy implementation and other changes at the national level. We can then have some basis for comparison across jurisdictions. Finally, there is often little understanding of the relationship between sending and receiving nations within East Asia and asylum seekers' countries of origin. The data presented here gives us a clearer empirical picture of these issues. The raw data is from the UNHCR, so Taiwan is not included. Macau's numbers were negligible. Data for Mongolia was not available until 2006.

2.1 Asylum Applications

Although the number of recognized refugees remains low in East Asia, asylum applications in the region have increased steadily and dramatically over the last twenty years (see Figure 1). Most of the increase in asylum applications has been in Japan and South Korea, but Hong Kong also experienced a steady flow of applications, which only began to decline in 2014. Asylum applications in East Asia first began to grow after September 11, 2001, at a time of deepening democracy in the region, as demonstrated by a significant growth in and strengthening of civil society and public interest law organizations advocating for refugees. These developments led to the most significant changes in refugee policy in the region: Japan's resettlement program, South Korea's Refugee Act and resettlement program, and Hong Kong's uniform status mechanism. These developments will be covered in more depth below.

2.2 Recognized Refugees

Figure 2 shows the number of refugees recognized in China, Japan, South Korea, Hong Kong, Macau, and Mongolia for each year from 2001 through

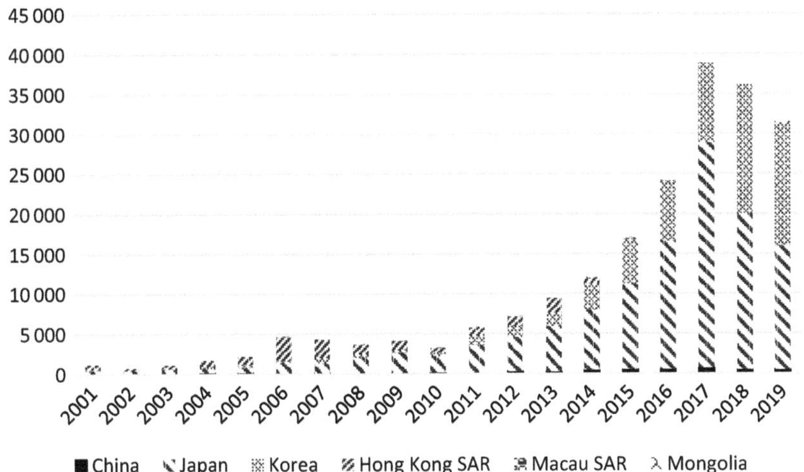

Figure 1 Asylum Applications 2001–2019.
Compiled using data from the UNHCR https://www.unhcr.org/refugee-statistics/download/?url=G6a4tv, last accessed May 7, 2021.

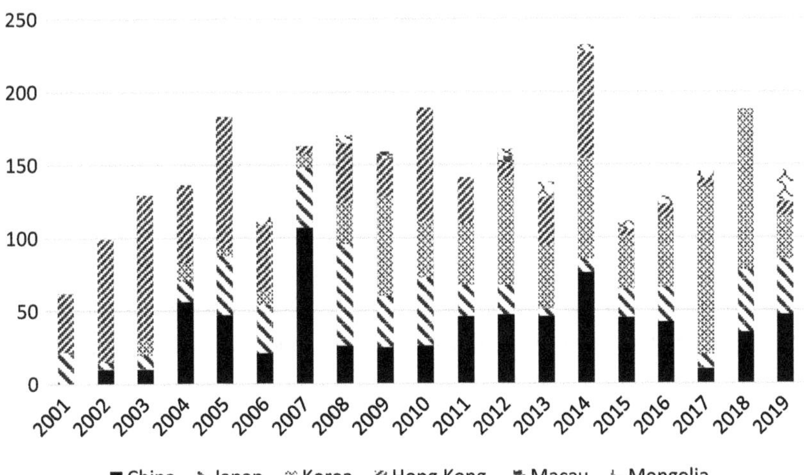

Figure 2 Recognition Decisions 2001–2019.
Compiled using data from the UNHCR https://www.unhcr.org/refugee-statistics/download/?url=G6a4tv, last accessed May 7, 2021.

2019. Despite the increasing number of asylum applications in East Asia, the number of those granted refugee status remains low. Even though applications surpassed 1,000 per year in Japan in 2006 and South Korea in 2011 and reached a high of over 28,000 in Japan in 2017 and over 16,000 in South Korea in 2018, recognition decisions have *never* reached 100 in Japan, and in South Korea, recognition decisions peaked at 110 in 2018. Even so, South Korea has consistently had some of the highest recognition numbers in East Asia since it surpassed Japan in 2009 – this was not difficult given that Japan received 2,594 applications that year and recognized thirty-five people as refugees. Two other interesting trends illustrated by Figure 2 are the high numbers of recognition decisions made by the UNHCR in Hong Kong and China. In China, asylum applications and decisions are handled by the UNHCR office in Beijing. Asylum seekers must make it to Beijing to apply; if they are recognized, they are resettled in other countries. Hong Kong is not a party to the Refugee Convention, but until recently, the UNHCR received and evaluated asylum applications. In addition, Hong Kong does offer protection based on its obligation to protect individuals from refoulement under the International Convention for Civil and Political Rights and the Convention Against Torture. These two programs were unified under its Unified Status Mechanism (USM) established in 2014. The USM will be discussed in more detail below.

The high numbers of applicants and the low numbers of those granted recognition are troubling; they indicate that a large majority of those in need of protection are not receiving it and remain vulnerable, especially if they are returned to their countries of origin. Such low numbers of recognized refugees also suggest the need to reevaluate refugee status determination policies and procedures. Cases such as China and Mongolia, where the UNHCR conducts status determination, suggest that these procedures are qualitatively different when undertaken by UNHCR protection officers using the organization's RSD procedures. The same holds for Hong Kong prior to 2015 when UNHCR conducted status determination there. After the universal status mechanism went into effect and UNHCR was relieved from RSD, the numbers recognized in Hong Kong significantly declined. It offers a sharp contrast to the outcomes of RSD carried out in Japan and South Korea by local immigration officers under national status recognition policies and procedures.

2.3 Sending and Receiving in East Asia

Japan and South Korea are major refugee-receiving states in East Asia. North Korea and China are major sending states. Hong Kong has been both a sending and receiving territory, and after the crackdowns on democracy activists in 2018–2020, it has been a net-sending jurisdiction. If Taiwan had a status determination system in place, it would also receive significant numbers of applications for refugee status, given the heavy flows from China and Hong Kong. Japan receives refugees from all over the world – Asia, Africa, the Middle East – but most of the refugees from 2001 to 2004 were from Turkey, mainly Turkish Kurds. In 2005, refugees from Myanmar became the largest group seeking protection in Japan. This remained the case until 2013, when refugees from Turkey again became the number one group, followed by those from Nepal as a close second. In 2019, the most recent year for which there is this kind of data available from the UNHCR, the largest number of people seeking protection in Japan was from Sri Lanka.

From 2001 until 2005, most of those seeking refugee status in South Korea were from China. In 2006 and 2007, the largest group was from Nepal. In 2008, those from Sri Lanka constituted the largest number of people seeking refugee status in South Korea. In 2009–2011, people from Pakistan constituted the largest number of people seeking refugee status in South Korea. In 2020, the most recent year for which UNHCR data for South Korea is available, most of the people seeking protection were from the Russian Federation. In Mongolia, the number of people seeking asylum is small; nonetheless, from 2006, the earliest year for which UNHCR data is available, until 2013, refugees seeking protection all came from China. In 2019, the most recent year for which there is UNHCR data, people seeking protection in Mongolia all originated from Turkey. In China, most of those seeking protection in 2002 were from Burundi; from 2003 to 2006, most of the asylum seekers in China originated in Pakistan. People coming from Iraq constituted the largest number seeking asylum in China from 2007 to 2010; those from Somalia took the position from 2011 to 2013. In 2020, the most recent year for which this information is available from UNHCR, the largest number of asylum seekers was from Cameroon (for these data and more, see unhcr.org/refugee-statistics [accessed April 24, 2023]).

2.4 Conclusion

The shifting international position of China from an underdeveloped communist country to an emerging market economy, of Japan from a postwar developing democracy to a fully developed economic powerhouse and strong democracy, and of South Korea from a developing authoritarian country to a developing democracy precipitated a shift in state interests and the institutionalization of the Refugee Convention in East Asia. The ten-year time period during which these three states ratified the Refugee Convention provided a specific context where all fit the description of middle powers interested in improving their international rank; their interests and identities might shift over time. In any case, East Asian acceptance of the Refugee Convention at this time is explained by constructivist theories of diffusion that uncover the role of state identity and international hierarchy in norm diffusion, as discussed above. The question of implementation is more complicated and began only after a long pause. Implementation has been uneven across all states and jurisdictions in East Asia where the Refugee Convention is in effect. Among these states, implementation is the least developed in China. Japan and South Korea's initial implementation focused on revising laws to include refugee recognition in immigration law. These two countries' historically strict immigration regimes (see Chung 2020 and Chung 2021) held a narrow definition of "refugee" and limited the number of refugees accepted. Implementation of the Refugee Convention is a politically contested process with uneven outcomes in these different jurisdictions. The remainder of the study will focus on the dynamic processes of implementation. The next section will discuss implementation, examine processes of international norm diffusion to the domestic level, and sketch out what this looks like in practice in East Asia with an initial examination of the highlights of developments in refugee protection in the region.

Many agents play a role in diffusing refugee protection norms and pushing for the implementation of refugee policy. These include lawyers, NGOs, IOs, government institutions, and refugees. To understand the politics behind the quantitative data presented in the previous section and the political processes driving refugee policy, it is important to understand who drives policy, who derails policy, how priorities are set, and the implications of those priorities. In each nation, there are complex politics of refugee acceptance that affect policy-making as well as implementation. For example, the decline in the number of asylum applications in Hong Kong probably reflects changes after the 1997 shift to "one country, two systems," when the territory ceased being a British colony and became a special administrative region of China.

Moreover, since China passed a new national security law for Hong Kong in June 2020 that curbs the autonomy of individuals and the territory itself, there has been an increase in the number of people leaving Hong Kong and seeking protection abroad. Some have even argued for Taiwan to establish refugee laws specifically for Hong Kong's political asylum seekers (Hung 2021). The data for China, which shows a relatively low number of applications for refugee status as well as low admissions, raises questions about the politics and policy around North Korean refugees fleeing to China. It suggests both that most North Koreans do not make it as far as the UNHCR office in Beijing, the only place where they can seek asylum, that most North Koreans interested in seeking protection probably do not opt to do so in China, and that those who do stay in China are not seeking the protection of refugee status. On the other hand, the relatively high recognition rate demonstrates UNHCR's responsibility for status determination procedures.

3 Drivers of Refugee Protection in East Asia

The early to mid-2000s was a period when East Asian nations had shifted from the initial phase of adopting the Refugee Convention and moved into a phase focused on implementing the norms of the Convention. Despite institutionalizing the Refugee Convention in much of East Asia, there was little implementation until 2001, when the first NGOs advocating for refugee rights in Japan emerged. Prior to the establishment of the Japan Association for Refugees, Japanese NGOs focused on refugee issues in Japan were service providers whose role was to assist refugees and asylum seekers; these organizations primarily dealt with material assistance. The Japan Association for Refugees was instrumental in forming the national network of NGOs working on domestic refugee issues, Refugee Assistance Japan (RAJA). This ushered in an era characterized by the emergence of advocacy NGOs in South Korea and Taiwan networking within East Asia and between East Asia and the broader Asia Pacific region. These transnational relations became denser with the establishment of the Asia Pacific Refugee Rights Network (APRNN). This networking organization was the first of its kind to connect NGOs working on refugee issues across all of Asia. The biennial meetings, Asia Pacific Refugee Rights Consultation, allow activists to meet in person. These Consultations are networking spaces where activists share local knowledge and advocacy strategies, and together, they develop alternative approaches to refugee protection that challenge the top-down international refugee regime with the Refugee Convention at its center (Choi 2020). According to Choi, this bottom-up approach moved away from focusing on institutionalization by convincing states to adopt the Refugee Convention to implementing refugee protection regardless of the status of the Convention in a given nation. For East Asia, this emerging emphasis on implementation reinforced and legitimized efforts on the ground in Japan and South Korea while providing alternatives for organizations in Taiwan (NGOs) and Hong Kong (law firms) that had no choice but to push for implementation without institutionalization since there is no possibility for adopting the Refugee Convention in those areas.

Nascent transnational networking between Japanese and South Korean NGOs gained momentum when the regional Asia Pacific Refugee Rights Network (APRRN) was formed in 2008, but networking in East Asia predates the formation of APRRN as indicated by a symposium organized by the Japan Association for Refugees with support from UNHCR Tokyo, Amnesty International Japan, and Japan Association of Refugee Lawyers. The daylong event, "Thinking About Refugee Protection Processes in Korea, New Zealand, and Japan," brought together NGOs from the three countries to discuss refugee recognition processes, asylum applications, and other issues. The development of APRRN, a regional network, has strengthened relations among groups in the region and East Asia specifically. In April 2008, the Sub-Regional Symposium on Refugee Protection in East Asia was co-organized by the Japan Association for Refugees and South Korea's Refugee pNan and held in Seoul under the theme of "Refugee Protection in East Asia and the Role of Civil Society." The East Asia working group of APRRN is led by NGOs from Hong Kong, South Korea, and Japan, with increasing participation of Taiwanese NGOs. In 2009, the Japan Association for Refugees hosted two conferences that highlighted a regional approach to refugee issues; these conferences brought together organizations from Japan, South Korea, and other countries in the region. These kinds of conferences provide essential venues for public education, information sharing, and both formal and informal networking.

3.1 Implementation and Global-Local Connections in Refugee Protection

Implementation – the creation of law and policy – does not necessarily follow institutionalization – treaty adoption, ratification, and associated processes. That gap has become an important area of research (Betts and Orchard 2014). Institutionalization and implementation, as Betts and Orchard (2014) argue, should be considered parallel processes, with institutionalization taking place at the international level and implementation at the domestic. Studying implementation allows us to understand how norms operate at the level of practice and to account for why norms change or are constrained in different contexts. Within Asia, the East Asian region is the leader in institutionalization, with most of the states in the region being parties to the Refugee Convention. However, implementation in the region is lacking. The gap between institutionalization and implementation illuminates the extent to which China (Choi 2017), South Korea (Lee 2014), and Japan (Flowers 2006, 2008, 2009) have adopted the Refugee Convention primarily to benefit the state with little concern for refugee protection and human rights. Implementation triggers a new phase of political contestation marked by ongoing processes whereby various actors, including NGOs, bureaucracies, lawyers, and other parties, shape norm diffusion, that is, the extent to which the Refugee Convention's protection norms are translated to the local level and how they are changed or constrained in that process (Betts and Orchard 2014). In East Asia, it is possible to detect tension between authoritarian tendencies, democratic challenges, and colonial legacies. This research demonstrates that "implementation may lead to different outcomes in terms of practice at the national, regional, and local levels and within different organizations" (Betts and Orchard 2014, 12).

Government action is necessary but not sufficient for implementing refugee protection. In East Asia, we have seen that NGOs, lawyers, and other non-governmental actors take the lead in implementation, and it is their initiative that pushes governments to create new policies or change existing policies to protect refugees. Advocacy for implementing the Refugee Convention was not limited to one nation but seemed to have been a wave carried around the region by transnational nonstate actors. Local, nonstate actors play a central role in leveraging global-local connections to advance the implementation of refugee protection. Localization (Acharya 2004), vernacularization (Merry 2006), and a global-local feedback loop (Tsutsui 2017) offer three ways to understand the relationship between international norms and local contexts. These diffusion processes are not mutually exclusive; each emphasizes different aspects but all address how actors on the ground work to spread norms domestically. Localization tends to emphasize actors' local knowledge and is a significant departure from scholarship that often privileged the role of Western norms gaining traction in non-Western contexts because of the moral superiority of these norms. Acharya's localization is based on observations in Southeast Asian states where international norms were not adopted wholesale but changed to suit the local context. Vernacularization centers actors' fluency in both international and local knowledge and highlights this fluency as expertise that sets actors apart from others with local knowledge. Merry clearly situates the action arena where translators learn norms in the international corridors of power at the United Nations. These actors then translate the international norms to the local arena. The norms are not translated wholesale but vernacularization requires tension between international norms and local practices to spur change at the local level. The global-local feedback loop emphasizes social movements over individual actors or other kinds of groups.

Implementation is a period of political contestation as different actors compete to gain leverage over the process in the interest of having their concerns addressed. This period is also characterized by ideational contestation since it is obligations from outside; in this case, those norms and ideas embedded in the Refugee Convention that may challenge or at least sit uneasily alongside domestic norms and ideas. So, how are international ideas made accessible and acceptable for a broad domestic audience?

One way that norms are made accessible and acceptable is through localization. Localization is a complex and dynamic process "whereby norm-takers build congruence between transnational norms and local beliefs and practices" (Acharya 2004, 241). In the localization process, even foreign norms that do not initially cohere with local beliefs and practices are incorporated into local norms. Opportunities for localization of these foreign norms are key for implementation. This conceptualization of international norm diffusion is a unidirectional process whereby norms move from the global to the local via local actors. Local actors' agency is central to this process as they are the ones who reinterpret and then reconstitute norms of protection to fit within existing domestic ideas. One of Acharya's primary contributions is the idea that international norms are not just grafted onto local norms as Price (1997) established. But these norms are also "pruned" or shorn of aspects that do not cohere with local norms and practices.

We see this localization process at play in Hong Kong, Taiwan, and Macau, for example. Their histories of sheltering dissidents, even if temporarily, provide a context where local practices and beliefs are amenable to norms of protecting refugees. In Hong Kong and Taiwan, this contributes to efforts on the ground to protect refugees from nonrefoulement despite not being party to the Refugee Convention. The politics around this issue in these three contexts also shapes localization.

One could argue that Japan and South Korea's approaches to protection also reflect a local preference for deciding who deserves protection and how they should be protected. The data presented later in Section 4 below shows a preference by Japanese and South Korean authorities to offer protection on humanitarian grounds instead of granting refugee status. This category of protection acknowledges that there is general support among the citizenry in Japan and South Korea to protect the most vulnerable based on conditions that are obviously and easily understood as humanitarian issues.

Vernacularization is a second process through which activists translate international norms to become meaningful to a domestic audience. This process focuses even more sharply on the agency of local actors as translators in the process of diffusing international norms to the local level: "Translators work at various levels to negotiate between local, regional, national, and global systems of meaning. Translators refashion global rights agendas for local contexts and reframe local grievances in terms of global human rights principles and activities" (Merry 2006, 39). Working on implementation where political contestation is a defining characteristic, translators are powerful and vulnerable as they negotiate this terrain of unequal power. Translators occupy a powerful position as they are knowledge brokers who have mastered legal and institutional discourses of both the domestic and international arena – in this case, the Refugee Convention. Nevertheless, the established domestic discursive terrain constrains translators. The most significant change is in those areas where the international norms challenge domestic norms enough to make noticeable progress from the status quo but do not offer too much of a challenge where they will be dismissed outright as incompatible with domestic beliefs and practices (Merry 2009). In addition to the degree to which domestic and international norms cohere, translators' positionality also shapes their work – their funding sources, social commitments, and institutional frameworks (Merry 2006, 40). One of the most interesting aspects of this theory of international norm vernacularization is Merry's conceptualization of international norms as norms that emerged elsewhere locally and traveled through transnational chains of translators that extend from one locality to another via international institutions.

The positionality of the translators draws our attention to how internal and external forces influence translators. Japanese activists' focus on human-rights-based arguments to advocate for refugee protection most clearly demonstrates vernacularization and the role of local translators in diffusing international norms domestically. These activists have a high level of expertise about the Refugee Convention, international refugee law, the situation in refugee-sending countries, and refugee policy worldwide. They also often have literal translation experience since many are fluent English speakers. They use their language skills in public education activities, which are important in creating broad public support for refugee rights and NGO activities.

Finally, the third process shifts the analytic focus from actor agency to the mutual constitution of global institutions and local social movements (Tsutsui 2017, 1050). Not only do global human rights constitute and reconstitute social movement actors by shaping how they understand the issues they work on but social movement actors also reinforce and even expand global norms (Tsutsui 2017, 1052). In other words, the global-local relationship goes in both directions, with local actors also influencing global norms and institutions. This global-local feedback is most visible in the transnational relationships between nonstate actors across Japan, South Korea, and Hong Kong. These relationships are formalized in the Asia Pacific Refugee Rights Network, the regional networking organization.

In Section 3.2, instead of presenting detailed individual accounts of China, Japan, South Korea, Hong Kong, Macau, Mongolia, and Taiwan, I will offer an overview of the status of refugee policy in the region by focusing on key developments, such as Japan's resettlement program, creation of Hong Kong's universal status mechanism, the response to Yemeni Refugees in South Korea, Taiwan's draft Refugee Act with the goal of illuminating implementation processes. We will notice that the three processes of norm diffusion outlined here are not mutually exclusive.

3.2 Implementation and Diffusion in Practice

As discussed above, *diffusion* is the process through which norms spread. It is a crucial link between institutionalization and implementation. Section 3.1 considered diffusion across states at the international level. In this section, the focus is on norms spreading from the global to the local level (and back) and becoming a part of the social and political context in a specific place. *Implementation* refers to how these norms are put into practice. The International Refugee Convention does not specify how states should implement the Convention. The most basic act of implementation is enacting refugee recognition laws that grant legal status. Yet, even this requires that norms be diffused locally to create support necessary to pass legislation. Field research in Japan, South Korea, Taiwan, and Thailand reveals that pressure from activists is essential for implementation. Activists are central in leveraging international norms and agreements to frame the issues locally and demand government action.

Japan and South Korea revised existing immigration laws to include refugees before ratifying the Convention, but implementation and the accompanying political contestation began in earnest in the early 2000s when activists decried the inadequacy of existing laws. In East Asia, implementing the Refugee Convention was not the result of governments taking steps to fulfill their international obligations. Indeed, the movement on implementation that we begin to see starting in 2001 resulted from demands made by civil society, lawyers, and other actors on the ground who began to use rights-based discourse to push their governments to protect refugees. Refugee advocacy organizations and lawyers working on refugee issues were emerging as essential proponents of implementation; they also helped raise the international profile of refugee protection in the region.

3.2.1 East Asia Outside of China: Japan, South Korea, Mongolia, and Taiwan

Diffusion of the norms codified in the Refugee Convention from the global to local level depends on groups and individuals who make new norms intelligible locally by translating them into a local vernacular and connecting somewhat familiar norms to existing local norms through localization. These diffusion processes can occur regardless of whether the government is a party to the Refugee Convention. It is important that there are actors on the ground who are committed to strengthening refugee protection and that they have the tools and conditions needed to create a culture where protection is valued. Who the actors are depends on the context and can include epistemic communities such as lawyers, nonstate actors such as NGOs, government officials such as local bureaucrats, local offices of international organizations such as the UNHCR, local branches of international NGOs (INGOs) such as Amnesty International, and other individuals interested in refugee protection. These actors use their skills, expertise, and networks to do this work, which can only be done in an open society that allows freedom of association and free speech.

Implementation is more likely in East Asian states with strong institutions, the rule of law, independent, active civil societies, and other conditions that create an environment conducive to the interactions necessary for norm diffusion. These are places where actors can engage in conferences and workshops, interact with government officials, and access international organizations. One example is a "Refugee Assistants Course" that JAR hosted, and the author attended during fieldwork in 2002–2004. The workshop brought together activists, people interested in learning about the refugee issue in Japan, lawyers, and people from the UNHCR Tokyo office over two consecutive Sundays for a total of nine hours. The goal was to educate the public on international refugee law and raise money for the organization. This workshop is an excellent example of how actors use public education to spread norms to a local audience. They used their network, including a membership list, to publicize the course. They used their connections with experts, including lawyers, officials at UNHCR Tokyo, and social workers, in addition to their own knowledge, as advocates for refugee protection for the substance of the course. There were no requirements or prerequisites to join; one only needed to pay the fee.

Japan, South Korea, and Taiwan have especially strong, nationally networked NGOs dedicated to working on refugee issues. In the case of Japan and South Korea, these organizations leverage their governments' commitments to the Refugee Convention in pushing forward their advocacy work. All of these states have local branches of Amnesty International. The local activists are involved in the organization's work on issues, including refugee protection and work to end torture and detention; they do the everyday work of localization and vernacularization on the ground. Given Taiwan's international position, civil society organizations have a high profile and play an important role in the nation's foreign policy, contributing to strong ties and significant interactions between NGOs and the government.

East Asian states outside of China have strong legal institutions. In Japan, South Korea, and Hong Kong, networks of activist lawyers with expertise on refugee issues also play a key role in implementation. All four of these territories are active in the Asia Pacific Refugee Rights Network (APRRN), a transnational network of NGOs, activists, scholars, lawyers, refugees, and others from East to West Asia. This network, its biannual meeting (the Asia

Pacific Refugee Rights Consultation APRRC), and regional and thematic working groups play a key role in norm diffusion to local levels as well (APRRC Bangkok, Thailand September 2–4, 2014; see also Choi 2020). Organizations and individuals from Japan, South Korea, Taiwan, and Hong Kong attend the East Asia working group. The APRRN is also involved in implementation, as a recent "Urgent Statement" from its website indicates. Visiting the organization's website on April 13, 2023, the reader is greeted with this statement: "The Asia Pacific Refugee Rights Network (APRRN) calls for the withdrawal of the amendment bill to the Immigration Control and Refugee Recognition Act (ICRRA) in its current form. We raise concerns that the bill, as approved by Japan's Cabinet on March 7, 2023, may result in longer periods in detention, lack of due process, and violation of the nonrefoulement principle." There is a button that invites readers to click for more information. The APPRN membership in East Asia consists of nineteen organizations and eight individuals – four organizations in Japan, two in Hong Kong, one in Taiwan, and nine in South Korea (aprrn.org [accessed April 13, 2023]). The APRRN facilitates the feedback loop that Tsutsui describes as it engages with the UNHCR and other UN organizations on behalf of network members and is a central node of norm diffusion and information sharing.

In Japan and South Korea, efforts to expand implementation started with advocates pushing for their governments to revise existing refugee policies and to create comprehensive refugee laws that address not only the legal status of refugees and asylum seekers but also their social and material well-being. Both countries saw the successive revision of their immigration laws, which governed refugee recognition, starting with strict time limits governing deadlines by which refugees had to submit applications for refugee status–either from the time they arrived in the country or from when the situation in their home country changed and fear of persecution made it impossible to return. Although such revisions appeared as small administrative changes, they resulted from painstaking work by NGOs. The emergence of these organizations marked a shift from the more traditional service-oriented civil organizations that had characterized civil society, especially in Japan (Flowers 2008). One advocacy organization, the Japan Association for Refugees, took a more proactive role in engaging the government. At the same time, the Japan Refugee Lawyers Association focused on challenging the government on refugee issues. Advocates used rights-based arguments rooted in international human rights law to make the case to support and protect refugees.

In South Korea, there was a similar process with two significant differences: the emergence of NGOs advocating for refugee rights was more directly related to South Korea's ongoing democratization, and lawyers were not just another set of actors involved in working on behalf of refugees – lawyers' groups and law firms actually constituted some of the advocacy organizations. In the most important breakthrough, South Korean civil society organizations that had worked for years on writing and lobbying the government to adopt legislation were successful in getting lawmakers to implement the Refugee Convention in a more substantial way than the piecemeal immigration policies had. The Refugee Act, albeit shorn of much of the rights-based language that characterized the initial draft, went into effect in 2013. For advocates, the Refugee Act represented a triumph in the region as it heralded the implementation of the Refugee Convention in a comprehensive national law for the first time. The broad coalition of civil society organizations, Korea's National Human Rights Commission, and the local office of the UNHCR successfully negotiated the domestic political terrain around the issue of refugees. Implementing the Refugee Act successfully moved the issue out of the adversarial realm of immigration issues, a realm dominated by concerns with state security, border control, and securitization of refugees and other foreigners (Choi and Park 2020, 6). However, as we will see later, the issue of securitization of foreigners – portraying a group of people as terrorists or criminal threats to national security – and securing foreigners' rights were not settled with the passing of the Refugee Act.

In a ground-breaking move, Japan was the first Asian nation to join the UNHCR's resettlement programs. The government, which has continued to resist calls from NGOs to establish a comprehensive refugee law, introduced a pilot resettlement program in 2007; the program was initially supposed to run for three years beginning in 2010. The goal was to resettle thirty refugees each year. In 2010, five families (a total of twenty-seven refugees) were resettled; in 2011, four families (eighteen refugees) were resettled. By 2012, the program had gained a reputation for being unresponsive to refugee needs when word of the difficulties of previously resettled refugees spread in Japan and in the camps where the refugees had originated; the three families (sixteen refugees) whom Japan had accepted for resettlement declined the offer, so no refugees were resettled in Japan that year. It was supposed to be the last year of the three-year pilot, and despite no refugee resettlement that year, Japan extended the pilot program for two more years. In 2013, four families (eighteen refugees) were resettled, and in the final year of the pilot program, 2014, five families (twenty-three refugees) were resettled in Japan. In 2015, the Japanese government made the resettlement program permanent (Lee 2018, 1224). Japan's resettlement program is the first in Asia and represents an important step in implementing the Refugee Convention domestically.

The Japanese government's approach to establishing the pilot program – insisting on maintaining tight control of all aspects of the program and shutting out the expertise of NGOs and refugees themselves – confirms that political contestation between and among actors on refugee issues in Japan has not changed much since advocacy organizations began pushing for change in the early 21st century. However, the weakness inherent in this approach threatened the future of the program. The government could not ignore the importance of activists and advocates for mobilizing their networks and using expertise to ease refugee transition to life in Japan if they wanted to address the shortcomings of their resettlement program. The government's initial approach demonstrates its control over creating and implementing policy. The failure of that policy led to engagement with nonstate actors with the expertise to help address the program's shortcomings.

Obligations to protect refugees challenge the fundamental understanding of the nation-state in East Asia, where ideologies of monoethnic nations have been used strategically as a central pillar of identity. The perception of foreigners and their (negative) social, political, and economic impact are taken for granted and have a significant impact on refugee policy. In the case of Japan's resettlement program, we see this perception at the core of policy. The initial program design excluded experts on refugee issues – civil society actors, lawyers, and refugees – and was limited to one ethnic group from Myanmar – the Karen – who were residing in the Mae La refugee camp on the Myanmar/Thai Border. The program sought to resettle nuclear family units with minor children. It prevented families from sponsoring other members, such as grandparents and older unmarried children, for residency in Japan at a later date.

The first three groups of refugees resettled in Japan via this program were settled outside urban areas and away from refugee communities who could ease their transition to life in Japan. The government decided that a rural place of settlement was best because they expected that rural areas of Japan would provide more opportunities for ethnic Karen to support themselves by engaging in agricultural labor, which was familiar to them from both Myanmar and the refugee camps. The exclusion of civil society, refugees, and others from resettlement planning meant the government planners had significant blind spots in their resettlement plan. They failed to account for the differences in farming that the refugees were used to in Myanmar and the camps where they farmed in the morning, avoiding the hottest part of the day. The more labor-intensive farming in Japan required long hours of work in hothouses. The rural location also meant that the roundtrip commute to take children to and from school could take more than four hours daily. The decisions that contributed to the program's failure prioritized preserving social cohesion. Hatcher and

Murakami (2020) argue that these kinds of policies are embedded in racism that underpins immigration policy in Japan in general and refugee policy in particular. These challenges eventually led the government to include input from NGOs representing groups of Burmese already in Japan and to allow their participation in supporting those who arrive in Japan via this resettlement program.

In March 2022, the Japanese government announced that it would accept Ukrainians fleeing the war between Ukraine and Russia. At first glance, this announcement suggested a significant change in Japan's refugee policy; activists and experts on Japan's refugee policy debated the impact of the decision. The decision would have limited impact as it would apply only to Ukrainians who have family members currently living legally in Japan. Moreover, the government would not accept fleeing Ukrainians as refugees but was instead considering creating a special quasi-refugee status to regularize their stay. The government eventually shelved this plan. Even so, the basis on which Ukrainians who would qualify would be accepted is a question related to complementary protection, which will be discussed in Section 4 below.

South Korea's 2013 Refugee Act marked a significant milestone toward implementing the Refugee Convention – both in the country and the region. The law resulted from a year-long negotiation process between the government and a broad coalition of civil society actors, lawyers, UNHCR, and others. This negotiated legislation was a triumph for democratic processes. It signaled a move away from stalemate and the all-or-nothing calls for change that had characterized contests between government and civil society in East Asia.

The Refugee Act established the legal basis for resettling refugees in South Korea. It explicitly authorizes resettlement of people recognized as refugees by the UNHCR but who need permanent places to settle. South Korea's pilot program, like Japan's, focused on resettling refugees from the camps on the Thai/Myanmar border. The pilot program ran from 2015 to 2017, during which time it resettled eighty-six refugees. In preparing the program, the government closely studied Japan's pilot program, and the Ministry of Justice organized a "Working Group on Resettlement" comprising government agencies, non-governmental organizations, international organizations, and municipal governments. Including civil society actors from the beginning contrasts with Japan's approach to creating its resettlement program. Such an inclusive approach resulted in an innovation in South Korea's criteria for resettlement compared to Japan's: it did not exclude the possibility of a family unit also bringing extended family members such as siblings, cousins, grandparents, aunts, uncles, and others. Although candidates for resettlement were not limited to one ethnic group, the government did initially focus on members of the Karen ethnicity (UN High Commissioner for Refugees (UNHCR), *Review of the pilot resettlement programme in the Republic of Korea*, December 2017, available at: https://www.refworld.org/docid/5ab25c2f4.html [accessed 2 April 2023]).

Despite the success of a broad coalition in getting the law passed, the Refugee Act faced criticism and calls for repeal in 2018, when a large number of Yemeni refugees arrived on Jeju Island, a South Korean tourist destination. These calls for repeal were accompanied by a petition with 700,000 signatures demanding that the government deport the refugees and pull out of the Refugee Convention (Choi and Park 2020, 14). This challenge demonstrated the continued importance and entrenched nature of the perception of security rooted in the mono-ethnic nation ideal and large numbers of foreigners presenting an existential challenge. Choi and Park (2020) compare the case of approximately 600 Syrian refugees being granted refugee status in South Korea without much notice in 2015, three years before the arrival of approximately 500 Yemeni refugees on Jeju Island in 2018. The latter was framed as a "mass influx" as the asylum seekers, mostly men, arrived within a short time frame on an island, not in an urban area. This "mass influx" resulted in serious public opposition to the Refugee Act. Choi and Park (2020) suggest that despite the broad coalition of actors involved in negotiating the Refugee Act, these NGOs, the local UNHCR office, and the National Human Rights Commission constituted an elite group with expertise in the area. This expertise creates a worldview informed by a commitment to human rights that may not be shared broadly, or that may be secondary to the ideology of a monoethnic society for the broader population (e.g., Lee 2009; Lie 2015; Lie 2001; Lie and Weng 2020; Murphy-Shigematsu 1993).

Until the end of the Cold War, Mongolia was within the Soviet Union's sphere of influence. It is now a democratic country with developing legal, political, and economic institutions, a developing but still small and weak civil society, and growing ties with Western liberal democracies. Since the late 1990s, Mongolia has sought to establish itself as a significant player in regional and global politics. Its position in a very complicated geopolitical region heightened the need to use alliances to maintain stability and independence. The United Nations considers Mongolia part of the East Asian region, but it sits at the crossroads of some of the most contentious geopolitical issues of the present day. As a response, Mongolia has established itself as a mediator in conflicts. It enjoys a position of trust in some of the most complex issues, including relations on the Korean peninsula (Hong 2022). It also has close bilateral ties with both China and India and is a part of Japan's free and open Indo-Pacific strategy (Mendee et al. 2022). At the international level, Mongolia has used the UN to establish its legitimacy in the rules-based liberal international order. To this end, the government has moved to institutionalize some of the core international human rights treaties. Its 1992 constitution established the possibility of granting asylum to people persecuted for their beliefs or political activities but did not establish a legally recognized refugee status. So, if authorities grant a person asylum, their lack of legal status means that they are, in fact, treated as an irregular migrant without a work permit. Its 2010 "Law on the Status of Foreign Citizens" reinforces access to asylum with a clear statement that "foreign nationals shall have 'the right to seek political asylum'" (UN High Commissioner for Refugees (UNHCR), *Submission by the United Nations High Commissioner for Refugees For the Office of the High Commissioner for Human Rights' Compilation Report- Universal Periodic Review: Mongolia*, September 2014, available at: https://www.refworld.org/docid/553a28474.html [accessed 14 March 2023]). The problem, of course, is the lack of a status determination process or standard for granting asylum. This procedural gap is where the UNHCR plays a role similar to what it does in China and has done in the past in South Korea, Japan, and Hong Kong before these jurisdictions had established their status determination procedures. Given the significant role that civil society organizations have played in refugee support and advocacy in other Asian countries, a freer society that allows for more robust non-governmental organizations could bolster the Mongolian government's institutionalization and implementation of refugee protection, irrespective of whether or not it ratifies the Refugee Convention. Evolution in this direction would also provide cover if China lodges complaints and pressures the Mongolian government to turn away Chinese asylum seekers. Closer coordination with the UNHCR, especially on status determination and resettlement, would also help to ease tensions that might arise around this issue.

Mongolia is not a party to the Refugee Convention, but it does allow the UNHCR to document, register, and conduct status determination for asylum seekers within its territory. The UNHCR provides asylum seekers with living assistance as well. As a small state with limited power in a complex geopolitical neighborhood, Mongolia operates in a vastly different context than China, South Korea, and Japan when they institutionalized the Refugee Convention. The hesitation to institutionalize the Refugee Convention highlights a challenge that all states in the region face – that is, how to avoid antagonizing powerful neighbors who are the source of refugees in the region. Mongolia and other states in the region need to balance refugee recognition without antagonizing China, a major refugee-sending country in the region. Amnesty International reported that not only had the Mongolian government deported two Chinese asylum seekers, the report noted that one of these people had a refugee status determination case pending with UNHCR (Amnesty International, *Amnesty*

International Report 2014/15 – Mongolia, 25 February 2015, available at: https://www.refworld.org/docid/54f07dc36.html [accessed 14 March 2023]). This is a clear case of refoulement. The UNHCR's Universal Periodic Review of Mongolia in 2014 found that cases like the deportation of the two Chinese asylum seekers that occurred earlier that year demonstrate that Mongolia's bilateral obligations overrule the informal system it has of allowing temporary stays until after status determination was complete and durable solutions for cases were found (UN High Commissioner for Refugees September 2014).

Although Taiwan has a precarious international status, it is a leader of democracy and human rights in East Asia; these are central to Taiwan's identity and distinguish it from mainland China (Krumbein 2019; Kironska 2022). Taiwan has a history of protecting refugees. In the 1960s, Taiwan sent warships to evacuate Chinese Indonesians who wanted to leave Indonesia during a time of ethnic conflict; the country also accepted about 6,000 Vietnamese starting in 1974. A draft law to deal with refugees and asylum seekers was first introduced in 2005. Drafts were also introduced in 2011 and 2012, but no action was taken. These three drafts included both Chinese nationals and other foreigners. When the Democratic People's Party (DPP) regained power in 2016, four more proposals to create a law were introduced; this time, they excluded Chinese nationals (Hung 2021; Kironska 2022). No law is forthcoming, and it is not clear what domestic institutions will emerge as central to refugee protection. However, one thing that distinguishes Taiwan from both Japan and South Korea is that the National Immigration Agency (NIA) responsible for refugees and immigrants is not situated in the Ministry of Justice but in the Ministry of the Interior (MOI).

Furthermore, Taiwan's NIA was newly formed in 2007; thus, the organizational culture had not yet become entrenched. This difference in where an authority on immigration in general and refugees in particular resides within the government is certainly important, but the significance remains unclear. There is some concern that the NIA will not be able to balance its responsibility to enforce the law and protect human rights. Some of these concerns are based on the widespread belief that a significant number of the NIA personnel are former National Police Agency (NPA) officials (Author interview. April 11, 2012, Taipei, Taiwan). Situating the NIA in the Ministry of Interior and charging them with the protection of trafficked persons and refugees introduce agency differentiation into a process that is the responsibility of the Ministry of Justice in Japan and South Korea. The case of Taiwan serves as a reminder that in addition to horizontal regional coordination, vertical coordination between subnational, national, and international levels is also required to address refugee issues adequately.

The proposed Refugee Act is part of the government's focus on human rights as a central pillar in Taiwan. The first change of the governing political party in Taiwan occurred in 2000, when the Kuo Min Tang (KMT) lost control of the government to the Democratic Progressive Party (DPP). The president initiated efforts to establish human rights as the organizing principle of Taiwan's policy perspective, and the government began to adopt UN human rights conventions and establish a national human rights commission and a legal framework to recognize refugees. These moves are instrumental in that the international human rights regime is one of the most powerful sources of state legitimacy; being a member in good standing would contribute to Taiwan's international position, especially important for a state that does not enjoy formal diplomatic relations with the main international players such as the United States and Japan. The efforts were also meant to gain favor with key domestic audiences. The symbolic power of the first election with a transition of power to the opposition, resulting in increased human rights protections, has broadened the appeal of the DPP. Some say that President Chen focused on human rights policy because many of his party members had been blacklisted in the past, and he did not want to recreate the history of Taiwan as a refugee-sending country – in other words, a country that exiled, exported, or otherwise cajoled political adversaries to leave the country. Although the Refugee Act was proposed under President Chen (DPP), his party never had enough legislative votes to enact it during his eight years in power. When the KMT returned to power with the election of President Ma, Ma continued to pursue human rights legislation. One expert in international human rights law explained that "domestically, these kinds of human rights policies have become a part of Taiwan's values, so [Ma] almost had no choice. There was also competition between Chen and Ma. Ma wants to be better than Chen. In any case, he doesn't want to be worse than Chen" (Author interview, professor of international human rights law, Taipei, Taiwan, April 11, 2012).

Sometimes, a jurisdiction like Taiwan cannot ratify an international agreement. However, it still has an institutionalization process that includes approving the agreement in the national legislature. This process precedes establishing domestic laws to implement international agreements. Attending to the institutionalization of the Convention in East Asia is important because it offers such a stark contrast to the broad resistance to the Convention in most of Asia. Taiwan's international position means that it has no formal relationship with the UNHCR but its government is exceptionally driven to adopt international human rights standards. Two examples are the International Convention on Civil and Political Rights and the International Convention on Economic Social and Cultural Rights, which were ratified and then implemented into domestic law – when the government attempted to deposit instruments of ratification at the UN, they were not accepted since Taiwan is not a member. One scholar of international human rights law described the two possible processes by which the government establishes human rights law in Taiwan: one is to ratify the relevant international agreement and incorporate the norms codified there into domestic law; the second is to create domestic law without an effort to incorporate the international standard. In his view, the first approach is the best because "it is important to include international standards … and because Taiwan's unique international position [the People's Republic of China is recognized by the United Nations and most states as 'China'] makes it a good way to prepare to be a part of the international community" (Author interview, Taipei, Taiwan, April 11, 2012). Thus, despite no official connection with UNHCR, the UN and its agencies still impact government action and civil society in Taiwan.

The fact that Taiwan's government had drafted a Refugee Act without adopting the Refugee Convention was seen as problematic (Author interview, Amnesty International Taiwan, Taipei, Taiwan, April 10, 2012; Author interview, Taipei, Taiwan, April 11, 2012), and the fact that the proposed Refugee Act did not incorporate the international standard provided significant motivation for Taiwanese NGOs to link up with the transnational refugee-advocacy network in Asia. Their goal is to ensure Taiwan's government commits to and complies with the Convention. When states ratify an international agreement through the UN, an important part of institutionalization is the periodic reviews. UN review processes also encourage NGOs and other civil society actors to participate by submitting counter- or shadow reports to offer information not included in government reports; they also remind governments to consult with NGOs when preparing official country reports. These processes that involve NGOs also contribute to diffusion processes as these actors use their knowledge, further develop their expertise, and apply the international standard to the local context in the process of deeply engaging with international agreements to understand their government's obligations. They use this knowledge to evaluate government progress on implementation and build it into their activities. Since Taiwan does not undergo such reviews under the relevant UN committees, it periodically invites international groups to undertake such reviews of how well the government is implementing the ICCPR and other international human rights agreements. A review in 2013 recommended that Taiwan's government establish refugee protections and mechanisms to grant political asylum to comply with the nonrefoulement obligations in the ICCPR (Kironska 2022).

The UNHCR has offices in Japan, South Korea, and Hong Kong and has previously provided RSD for these jurisdictions before they developed their procedures for conducting status determination. However, Taiwan has no official government connections with the UNHCR, so the refugee organization is allowed to maintain relations with and assist NGOs in Taiwan. Given that Taiwan does not yet have a refugee recognition system or RSD procedures, the relationship between Taiwanese NGOs and UNHCR will shape how these organizations understand status determination. The experience of Japanese and South Korean NGOs and their relationships with local UNHCR offices are instructive. In Japan and South Korea, the local UNHCR office has played a significant role in capacity building among NGOs and government officials alike. NGOs will then help to translate and localize these norms through their interactions with other stakeholders, such as government officials, local bureaucrats, local activists, and community members. Although the UNHCR no longer conducts RSD in Japan and South Korea, it still plays a key role in strengthening protection through capacity building. For example, the UHNCR Seoul office hosted meetings between NGOs, government officials, and others that led to the Refugee Act (Author Interview, UNHCR Seoul, South Korea 2010). The UNHCR Tokyo facilitated monthly meetings of Japanese NGOs working on refugees within Japan and abroad, eventually spawning a domestic NGO network, Refugee Assistance Japan (RAJA), and Japan Platform, a network of Japanese NGOs working on refugee issues abroad, funding organizations including Keidanren, the Ministry of Foreign Affairs and others (Flowers 2008).

3.2.2 China and Its SARs

China is a long-established authoritarian regime with repressive policies that limit civil society activity, increasingly antagonistic relations with the major liberal democracies, and centralized control over institutions. Although China institutionalized the Refugee Convention the same year as Japan, it has not made meaningful progress toward implementing it. Moreover, its repressive regime does not have the political space for norm diffusion. No NGOs publicly work on refugee issues in China (Song 2020b). The UNHCR has an office in Beijing, but the lack of NGOs working on refugee issues in China severely limits the possibility for norm diffusion through vernacularization and localization. In other East Asian jurisdictions where the UNHCR has a presence and/or has been charged with conducting RSD, the organization built a strong rapport with government officials, especially those in ministries of justice and foreign affairs (Author Interview, UNHCR Seoul, South Korea; Tokyo, Japan). The local UNHCR offices have used these connections to help build state capacity by holding workshops for these government officials and through regular consultation; such iterative interactions also serve to diffuse norms. In other states, the UNHCR has also contributed to networking among civil society organizations and between these organizations and the government. The absence of an independent civil society in China is also evident here.

The politics around refugee acceptance in the region demonstrates that concerns around managing relations with China seem to have impacted how others in the region – both with formally established protection systems such as Japan and those working to establish systems such as Taiwan – respond to Chinese asylum seekers. In Japan, the first Chinese asylum seeker was granted refugee status after an eight-year wait. Local activists viewed this long delay in recognition as the result of political concerns. We saw how concern about cross-strait relations has contributed to a lack of progress on Taiwan's Refugee Act; Taiwan does not relish the possibility of provoking China by recognizing Chinese asylum seekers as refugees. Suppose Taiwan established a Refugee Act with recognition procedures and a status determination process. In that case, there is no doubt that asylum seekers from mainland China and Hong Kong would be among those seeking protection. If a state with the power and standing of Japan is reluctant to create friction by recognizing Chinese refugees, Taiwan certainly wants to avoid that possibility. Hong Kong was in a similar position. The British declined to extend its obligations under the Refugee Convention to Hong Kong to avoid having to recognize Chinese refugees, and the Hong Kong SAR government opted to keep this status quo after the transition. Despite creating a status determination system, Hong Kong has continued to deny resettlement. We might speculate that similar concerns are at play in Macau's failure to recognize refugees despite having created a robust recognition system. While China casts a long shadow over refugee recognition in other East Asian jurisdictions, it is not immune to (geo)political concerns in handling refugee issues. Although the government tolerates North Koreans crossing the border into China, they engage in a delicate balancing act to deter mass exits from the DPRK.

China's special administrative regions, Hong Kong and Macau, exercise independence over some areas of governance, including immigration and refugees. Each has inherited political cultures and legal systems from their former colonial powers, and each has adapted differently to the one-country, two-systems approach. In the years since their status change in 1997 and 1999, respectively, China has exerted more control and curbed freedoms. Macau's political culture, weak civil society, and lack of political opposition are similar to China's. When power over the affairs of these two island nations reverted to China in the late 1990s, the status of the Refugee Convention in both places was one of the issues that had to be dealt with explicitly during preparations for the transition (Song 2020). As both territories retained significant control over immigration issues – including refugee protection – the status of refugees quickly became an issue that needed to be resolved.

Hong Kong was under the United Kingdom's rule from 1842 until July 1, 1997, and Macau was under colonial rule by Portugal from 1557 until December 20, 1999. The status of the Refugee Convention and subsequent developments in refugee protection in these two special administrative regions of the People's Republic of China were the legacy of colonial rule. Although both Hong Kong and Macau had historically provided refuge to displaced mainland Chinese at different times (Song 2014, 2020), they took very different approaches to implementing the Refugee Convention. Portugal extended its obligations under the Refugee Convention to Macau in 1999. The UK never extended its obligations under the Refugee Convention to Hong Kong, and the Hong Kong administration strongly objected to having China's obligations under the Refugee Convention extended to the territory after July 1, 1997. When Hong Kong and later Macau came under China's control with "one country, two systems," the two special administration regions retained sovereignty over immigration issues within their respective territories; that meant each was free to establish legal and policy frameworks to implement refugee protection.

Despite having the same institutional arrangements under "one country, two systems," China's two SARs have distinct state-society relations and political cultures shaped by relations between China and the two colonial powers, Britain and Portugal. The China-Britain relationship was adversarial, while the Portuguese assimilated more to local Chinese norms, and China had more of an influence on the governing process in Macau (Chun 2019, 422). The relatively weak association with Portugal and strong political and cultural attachment to China smoothed repatriation, and Macau residents readily embraced a Chinese national identity. Macau's public has steadily expressed trust in both the local SAR government and the national government in Beijing since repatriation. Indeed, trust in the national government is 50 percent (Wong and Kwong 2020). There has been broad social stability due to this relatively high trust in the government and strong support for Beijing, where pro-Beijing politicians receive 60 percent support. Opposition parties and civil society groups are weak. Social mobilizations are not common in Macau, and when they do occur, they usually target specific government policies; they do not demand broad political reform, democracy, or free speech. So, popular dissatisfaction is not a direct challenge to mainland government and governance (Ieong and Wu 2021).

Between 1978 and 1991, Macau hosted about 40,000 Vietnamese refugees in camps. Since then, Macau has received only a few applications for refugee status. In 2004, Macau established a law, the Regime of the Recognition and Loss of Refugee Status, to implement the Refugee Convention and establish a refugee status determination system (Song 2020). A Refugee Affairs Commission in Macau assesses applications for refugee status and recommends whether to grant refugee status. The policy sets out strict timelines for assessing the application, but in reality, they are not met, and it could take up to eight years to process an application (Song 2020, 165). In the case of a mass influx of refugees, the system allows Beijing to become involved. Despite establishing refugee status determination (RSD) procedures in 2004, Macau has not recognized any refugees.

In contrast to Macau's embrace of a Chinese national identity, Hong Kong residents have a very strong local Hong Kong identity that sits in opposition to a Chinese national identity; the balance of whether Hong Kong residents identify as Chinese or as Hong Kongers has shifted drastically since repatriation, in June 2019, more than 50 percent self-identified as Hong Kongers, while those who identified as Chinese hit a low of 10 percent (Wong and Kwong 2020). In Macau, 80 percent of the population has consistently identified as Chinese. This suggests the difficulty that people in Hong Kong have had adopting a national identity and reconciling it with their local identity. This Hong Kong identity is closely tied to a distinct political culture defined by a more free and open society and democratic values. The strong local identity contributes to political mobilization, where a strong civil society pushes for broad democratic reforms. The local population uses social movements to express their preferences and dissatisfaction with government policies, undemocratic local government, and Beijing's interference in local governance (Wong and Kwong 2020; Ieong and Wu 2021). After repatriation, there remained strong opposition parties in Hong Kong politics that matched the strength of pro-Beijing parties and politicians, leading to much more political contestation than in Macau.

Another difference between Hong Kong and Macau is the legal culture. While Macau's courts "tend to apply legal reasoning consistent with government policy" (Ieong and Wu 2021, 670), Hong Kong has a vibrant legal community. Lawyers' expertise has been central to the evolving refugee policy in Hong Kong. When three court cases challenged the fairness of Hong Kong's system, lawyers emerged as the central actors shaping how the Refugee Convention would be implemented in Hong Kong. As the cases progressively implemented the norm of nonrefoulement of both refugees and (potential) victims of torture, the role of the UNHCR and Hong Kong administrators was redefined, with the latter becoming more influential in determining how protection mechanisms functioned. The steady erosion of Hong Kong's civil society and political culture makes it reasonable to expect that space to debate these issues will continue to narrow over time.

3.3 Conclusion

Despite Japan, South Korea, and China institutionalizing the Refugee Convention in the early 1980s and 1990s, there remained a significant gap between institutionalization and implementation in each country. Motivated by state interests and identity, governments took the initiative in institutionalization. However, they had no incentive to implement the Convention any further than their initial efforts that followed soon after adopting it. Further implementation would not be realized until NGOs in Japan and South Korea began advocating for change. Change has typically been piecemeal, coming in fits and starts. This was not surprising given that refugee protection challenges state sovereignty and the fundamental identity of the nation, thus making instituting more significant laws and policies to protect refugees difficult. Analysis of China and its SARs and East Asian states outside of China shows that the strength and openness of institutions, rule of law, and free and open societies increase the opportunities for norm diffusion and implementation even if governments are initially resistant. Norm diffusion is necessary for implementation, and this process largely depends on local activists; without them, norm diffusion and implementation are nearly impossible. The next two sections will focus more keenly on implementation by examining two central policies related to refugee protection – refugee status determination and complementary protection.

4 Refugee Status Determination Procedures

Refugee status determination procedures are the most basic step in implementing refugee protection. It is also an area that clearly demonstrates the narrow space available for civil society influence even in democratic states. Whether and how states conduct RSD demonstrates how officials view refugees – whether they are people with rights deserving protection or a security threat to be managed. Civil society organizations can lobby the government to establish laws for legal recognition, and advocate for establishing RSD procedures; they can even suggest what kinds of protection is most humane but the process is under the government's control. In cases where RSD procedures already exist, civil society organizations can advocate for revisions to ensure the policies recognize and protect refugee rights more broadly.

Governments establish their own refugee status determination procedures to legally determine the status of people seeking asylum or protection under the Refugee Convention. Although a person might meet the Convention's definition of a refugee, states neither provide protection under their treaty obligations nor grant access to legal, economic, or social benefits unless and until their government officials formally acknowledge the refugee status of an individual or a group. RSD procedures reflect the state's interests. They are also a site where tensions become apparent between state sovereignty and the obligation to protect refugees. RSD procedures balance domestic and international interests and provide a window into how governments view refugees. In some cases, where states have been unwilling or unable to establish RSD procedures, the government might allow the nearest local or regional UNHCR office to conduct RSD.

Even if states ratify the Refugee Convention, domestic legislation and refugee status determination (RSD) procedures can violate or affirm the human rights of refugees and ensure the integrity of the Refugee Convention. These procedures reflect the relative balance between national interests and humanitarian concerns (Bari 1992). By comparing the RSD procedures of East Asian nations, we can see how they codify national interests and attitudes regarding refugees. One observation is that the procedures in East Asia reflect preoccupations with the enforcement of law and order, especially concerning immigration law and national defense and security; they also demonstrate little concern for applying international refugee law in a humanitarian way or for protecting refugees. For example, a negative attitude about refugees in Japan has fueled attempts to limit the number accepted. Before 2004, the government limited refugee recognition by using a strict time limit known as the "Sixty-Day Rule," which required asylum seekers to apply for refugee status within sixty days of arriving in Japan or from the date at which the situation in their country of origin made it impossible for them to return. Such a time limit bears no relation to the veracity of the claim of a well-founded fear of persecution, but it provided a basis for denying asylum claims.

The UNHCR recognizes the need for RSD to balance state interests with humanitarian protection and has established no strict standard that all RSD procedures must meet. The UNHCR does have a handbook to guide how its officers conduct RSD under the UNHCR's mandate in situations where "a country is not a state party to the Convention or the Protocol, have restricted the application of these instruments, or have yet to enact refugee legislation, or when their RSD procedures are non-functioning or do not meet minimum standards" (Simeon 2010). The UNHCR and its Executive Committee also publish guidelines to help address issues that arise during status determination, but states are not required to consult these handbooks and memoranda. Nevertheless, there is general agreement among scholars and practitioners that best practices for the design and administration of refugee status determination procedures include: (1) independence, including independent appeal, (2) consistency, and (3) competent decision makers (Simeon 2010). Although activists do not exercise any control over RSD, they do advocate for the government to work toward achieving these best practices.

Across East Asia, governments base RSD procedures on restrictive immigration policies that circumscribe who can enter the nation's borders, under what conditions, and for how long. Authorities may prohibit individuals from entering a country by strict pre-arrival immigration regulations, including visa requirements. Post-arrival, they may be subject to detention and removal policies that aim to exclude those very groups that often arrive as refugees in need of protection (Schloenhardt 2002). Immigration laws seek to exclude those authorities' view as threatening the country's economic, political, and social stability. Although some nations have revised their RSD procedures over time, of the East Asian countries that have instituted status determination procedures, without fail, initial procedures reflect the widely held view that those claiming to be refugees are actually economic migrants who have left their countries in search of a better life and should be excluded. The basis of their exclusion is the belief that they threaten the nation's economic health or social stability. In fact, one's life chances, including economic opportunity, are closely tied to the grounds upon which refugee claims are made (race, religion, nationality, membership in a social group, political opinion), and persecution is not defined in the Convention but has an evolving scope that certainly includes human rights violations, including being deprived of access to the means to live a life of dignity due to one's race, religion, nationality, and so forth (McAdam 2007; McAdam 2011).

Moreover, reasons for fleeing can include a well-founded fear of persecution as defined in the Refugee Convention *and* secondary reasons such as material deprivation, including access to basic human needs like food or education. Given that in some Asian countries, including Japan and South Korea, those tasked with executing RSD procedures are usually trained in immigration enforcement, it is important to shift their orientation to ensure that they can competently apply refugee law in a humanitarian manner (Bari 1992). Before we get in to how to facilitate that shift in orientation, let us examine RSD procedures more closely across East Asia.

Table 1 shows the percentage of applications recognized in East Asian nations; this is a better measure for comparative analysis than raw numbers. Considering the percentage of applications recognized allows us a better

Table 1 Percentage of Applications Recognized 2001–2019.

Year/Country	China	Hong Kong	Japan	Mongolia	S. Korea
2001	N/A	6.36	4.08		0
2002	33.33	30.21	1.08		0
2003	22.22	26.54	1.58		13.51
2004	37.08	6.76	2.32		8.88
2005	30.51	8.79	6.33		1.25
2006	23.86	1.49	2.45	50	3.67
2007	82.3	0.22	3.25	0	1.39
2008	92.85	3.28	3.33	100	7.86
2009	37.87	2.09	1.34	0	21.93
2010	16.66	13.35	2.24	0	9.2
2011	106.97	2.98	0.61	0	3.71
2012	18.57	0.82	0.49	71.42	5.42
2013	16.66	1.85	0.09	100	2.55
2014	16.66	10.48	0.13	83.33	2.07
2015	8.62	7.46	0.19	100	0.63
2016	7.85	100	0.15	100	0.62
2017	1.47	50	0.04	100	1.15
2018	7.2	N/A	0.22		0.68
2019	10.1	100	0.25	100	0.19

comparative measure for analysis. There is no globally agreed-upon way to calculate the refugee recognition rate. However, the UNHCR calculates a global recognition rate that includes all reporting states and UNHCR recognitions. In 2009, the global recognition rate was 38 percent (https://www.unhcr.org/4ce531e09.pdf accessed March 19, 2022). Table 1 shows that China's recognition rate was 38 percent; we must remember that China does not resettle refugees, and the UNHCR's local Beijing office handles its recognition procedures. South Korea's recognition rate for 2009 was 22 percent, and Japan had the lowest recognition rate of 1 percent . Overall, Japan has the lowest recognition rate of the four places represented on the tables. Its highest recognition rate reached 6 percent in 2005. China and Hong Kong, where the UNHCR handles refugee status determination, had the highest overall recognition rates. In some years, Mongolia also had very high rates.

The causes and consequences of recognition rates are many and vary from the availability of interpreters to government ideology to the identity of individuals deciding the cases. Even in the best cases, RSD procedures are rough and messy ways of determining who deserves protection. Ensuring all who need the protection that refugee status offers receive it means establishing easily accessible, fair, and robust RSD procedures that qualified professionals consistently apply. Governments can address high rejection rates by attending to three areas: access to counsel, transnationality of RSD, and governance of refugee law (Jones 2009). These three areas cut across all states and regions and are central to addressing high rejection rates; the first two are especially relevant for the present study. Access to counsel helps ensure that the RSD "outcome is based on full facts of the case and understanding of international law" (Jones 2009, 53).

In the regular course of carrying out these duties, legal counsel will advocate for applicants for refugee status to receive appropriate facilities, including interpreters, necessary to establish the facts of the case. Attention to the transnationality of refugee status determination is a fact in even the most basic cases, given that these decisions apply laws in one country to the circumstances of another to determine the fate of the person applying for refugee status. Training in refugee law, especially the unique transnational aspects of this body of law, its practice, and application, is lacking in contemporary legal education in most countries (Jones 2009). Finally, there is the issue of governance. "UNHCR must both develop refugee law, attempt to secure its application by states, and apply it in its own RSD operations" (Jones 2009, 54). It is no mistake that those jurisdictions that depend on the UNHCR for status determination more closely approximate the global recognition rate. Finally, because not 100 percent of the cases are resolved each year, there are times when the recognition rate can exceed 100 percent, such as China's in 2011. Some years, the number of cases accepted exceeds the number who applied because unresolved cases carry over into the next.

4.1 Refugee Status Determination by Country

After the Indochinese refugee crisis, China and Japan ratified the Refugee Convention and the 1967 Protocol. China adopted both the Convention and Protocol in 1982, while Japan adopted the Convention in 1981 and the Protocol in 1982. Forty years after ratifying the agreements, China has not yet established RSD procedures. Obligations under the Refugee Convention and Protocol extend to the Macau SAR but not Hong Kong SAR. Japan revised its immigration act to address refugee recognition. South Korea ratified the Refugee Convention and 1967 Protocol in 1992 and, like Japan, revised its immigration act to address how to recognize individual refugees officially. Because Taiwan is not a member of the United Nations, it cannot become a party to the Refugee Convention and Optional Protocol; Taiwan does not have refugee status determination procedures. Taiwan has, however, adopted the International Covenant on Civil and Political Rights (ICCPR), one of the core human rights agreements and one that prohibits refoulement. Civil society organizations advocate for refugee acceptance and protection, and a draft Refugee Act was initially introduced to the legislature in 2006 (author interview, Taiwan 2012). In 2009, Taiwanese NGOs became actively involved in revising the legislation and advocating for its passage (Choi 2019). Ten years later, Taiwan's Refugee Act still had not passed. Using the experiences of South Korean NGOs (all are APRRN members that contributed to drafting South Korea's Refugee Act and advocating its passage), APRRN's Legal Aid and Advocacy Working Group became involved in pushing Taiwan's legislature to pass the Refugee Act. As of this writing, Taiwan's Refugee Act has still not passed, and there have been increased calls for it since 2019 by supporters of democracy activists in Hong Kong.

4.1.1 China

China joined the international response to the surge of Vietnamese refugees by endorsing the Comprehensive Plan of Action (CPA), an international effort to standardize refugee status determination and share the burden of protecting and resettling Vietnamese refugees. Under this plan, the Chinese government resettled more than 250,000 Vietnamese refugees from 1978 to 1982. Nevertheless, RSD procedures and domestic implementation of the Refugee Convention are still lacking (Schloenhardt 2002; Song 2018). Since the mid-1990s, Chinese authorities, including the Ministry of Foreign Affairs, the Ministry of Public Security, and the Ministry of Civil Affairs, have been working on "Rules for the Identification and Administration of Refugees" with assistance from the UNHCR. After more than twenty years, it is clear that there has been no progress because the Chinese government has no interest in implementing RSD procedures. In 2008, a draft was finally presented to the Chinese State Council for consideration but has never been adopted (Song 2018, 148). In 2012, the Chinese government finally revised its Exit and Entry Administration Law, Article 46, which outlines the criteria for legal status for asylum seekers and lawful stays for refugees for the first time (Choi 2017, 232). However, there are still no clear and transparent RSD procedures.

The lack of RSD procedures reflects China's position that successfully addressing refugee flows requires addressing "root causes," which, for them, include poverty and underdevelopment. This view is based on China's experience as a source of refugees from the mainland to Hong Kong, a refugee flow that lasted from the establishment of the PRC in 1949 until the early 1980s.

Despite the heavy presence of the People's Liberation Army between Shenzhen and Hong Kong and the threat of death to deter those trying to flee, the flow continued. In the late 1970s, Deng Xiaoping argued that the economic gap between mainland China and Hong Kong was the main driver of refugees, and he focused on narrowing that gap by establishing a Special Economic Zone in Shenzhen City in 1979. Authorities attributed the sharp decline in the number of people trying to cross into Hong Kong in the early 1980s to the economic development of Shenzhen. It continues to influence government officials' view of why refugees flee and the most effective ways to address such movements (Song 2018, 141). Of course, the focus on economics and material conditions ignores the role of politics and the connection between the two in creating refugees. Because China lacks RSD procedures, the UNHCR regional office, established in 1997 in Beijing and covering mainland China, conducts refugee status determination under its mandate for those who make it to Beijing to seek protection. However, even this route is not open to everyone as the government maintains a no-admission policy for North Koreans and views ethnic Kokangs and Kachins from Burma/Myanmar as "special border residents" (Song 2017). The subregional office in Hong Kong covers Hong Kong, Macau, and Mongolia; it does RSD in Mongolia under the UNHCR mandate.

4.1.2 Macau

China's government extended the application of the Refugee Convention to Macau when Portugal ended its colonial rule over the region in 1999 and withdrew its extension of the obligation under the Refugee Convention and 1967 Protocol to Macau as a colonial holding (Schloenhardt 2002). To meet the obligations of the Convention, Macau implemented a law, "Legal Framework on the Recognition and Loss of Refugee Status," in 2004. This law established a commission to determine refugee status in the special administrative region (Song 2014, 93). The number of applications for refugee status and the recognition rate are both low in Macau despite the region's generous definition of "refugee." In addition, despite the low numbers of applicants, when there are applicants, the government has a difficult time processing applications within the time frame specified in the law. According to Song, "as of mid-2013, there were no refugees and only six asylum seekers residing in Macau. From 2002 to early September 2011, only 15 requests for refugee status were submitted, of which 10 were denied, and one was canceled" (Song 2014, 94). The case of Macau demonstrates that despite being a party to the Refugee Convention, having a comprehensive law regarding refugee status determination, and providing refugees the same rights as residents, it still suffers from delays in the process and the low recognition rate that seems to be a pattern in East Asia. Macau is the clearest case in East Asia that implementation without substantial diffusion leads to ineffective policy.

4.1.3 Hong Kong

In China's other special administrative region, Hong Kong, the situation surrounding refugee protection is much more complex and dynamic. In short, the Hong Kong government protects people from being sent back to places where they might face persecution, but the government neither recognizes nor accepts refugees. Unlike Macau, the Refugee Convention did not extend to Hong Kong. The British colonial authority never extended its obligations to Hong Kong under the Refugee Convention and Optional Protocol. If it had, they would have had to evaluate the status of people fleeing mainland China and extend protection. After repatriation, the local authorities resisted extending the Refugee Convention and 1967 Protocol in the special administrative region and have taken a strong position against granting asylum. When Hong Kong became a special administrative region of China, the local government retained control of immigration, including the power to establish laws regarding asylum seekers and refugees (Loper 2010, 405). Despite opposition to granting asylum, Hong Kong is still bound by seven core international human rights instruments that include implicit and explicit guarantees of nonrefoulement; these include the Convention Against Torture and Other Cruel, Inhuman, or Degrading Treatment or Punishment and the International Covenant on Civil and Political Rights, both of which inform constitutional rights in Hong Kong and have been implemented into Hong Kong law (Loper 2010, 405). These obligations are the basis for the continued evolution of Hong Kong's procedures that deal with asylum seekers. These commitments explain why, despite not being bound by the Refugee Convention, Hong Kong's court's legal decisions continue to require the government to protect people who will be subject to persecution and torture if they are deported, including but not limited to refugees.

Since the Hong Kong government resolved the last cases of Vietnamese refugees and the camps were closed in 2000, the Hong Kong government and the UNHCR subregional office in Hong Kong operated under an informal agreement that the UNHCR office would determine the status of refugees under the UNHCR mandate for people seeking protection from refoulement in Hong Kong. There are no legal provisions for refugees, but the Hong Kong government does allow refugees and asylum seekers to remain in Hong Kong until their cases are resolved. So, while waiting for their cases to be decided and/

or for resettlement in another country, asylum seekers and refugees have no legal status in Hong Kong; they cannot work and have no access to social services such as subsidized housing or income support.

Hong Kong courts decided a series of cases from 2004 to 2014 that led to establishing the unified status mechanism (USM) and completely changed how the Hong Kong government handled *nonrefoulement* claims, including those of refugees. In 2004, Prabakar, an ethnic Tamil from Sri Lanka, sought asylum based on a claim that he was tortured in Sri Lanka. The UNHCR initially denied Prabakar refugee status, and the Hong Kong government issued a deportation order. The government refused to rescind the order even after the UNHCR reversed its decision and granted Prabakar refugee status. Prabakar took advantage of Hong Kong law, allowing those denied refugee status to seek judicial review. The Hong Kong Court of Final Appeal found that "a person not protected by the Refugee Convention might nevertheless be protected by the Convention Against Torture (CAT) and vice versa" (Loper 2009; Song 2020, 146). The Court of Final Appeals decision in the *Prabakar* case essentially found that the UNHCR subregional office in Hong Kong's refugee status determination procedures was inadequate insofar as it did not provide for the protection of potential victims of torture who were not necessarily refugees (Loper 2009, 253) and led to the creation of a second, overlapping mechanism, the "torture screening mechanism," that essentially operated on a parallel track (Loper 2010, 407). The Hong Kong Immigration Department administered the torture-screening mechanism that allowed complainants to seek protection from refoulement to a country where they would be tortured; the claims are based on Article 3 of the Convention Against Torture. These overlapping and parallel tracks, RSD under the UNHCR and torture screening under the Hong Kong authorities, did not provide efficient and effective procedures to protect refugees, asylum seekers, and others needing protection. A 2008 decision by the Court of First Instance held that neither the torture screening mechanism nor the refugee screening mechanism met the "high standards of fairness" set out in *the Prabakar* case. The mechanisms continued to lack publicly funded legal assistance, did not allow legal representation at interviews, and there was insufficient training for decision-makers, among other things. In response, the torture-screening mechanism was revised in December 2009. That same year, the UNHCR and the Hong Kong government increased their level of cooperation to improve the training and expertise of immigration officers responsible for screening torture claims (Loper 2010). Another significant development in 2009 was that the Hong Kong government began providing publicly funded legal aid to all torture claimants after the 2008 decision by the Court of First Instance in the *FB* case that found that the policy of denying legal representation to torture claimants was illegal and did not meet the high standard of fairness required by Hong Kong's obligations under international agreements (Song 2020, 147).

Finally, in March 2014, a "unified screening mechanism" administered by the Hong Kong government was implemented to determine claims for nonrefoulement protection based on all applicable grounds, including those provided for in the Refugee Convention. Simultaneously, UNHCR stopped processing asylum claims. However, establishing the unified screening mechanism did not reverse the Hong Kong government's long-standing position against determining refugee status and granting asylum. "If a person's non-refoulement claim on the grounds of persecution risk is substantiated under the unified screening mechanism the person would be referred to UNHCR for recognition of refugee status," and the responsibility to resettle recognized refugees outside of Hong Kong would fall to the UNHCR (Song 2014, 94). Lawyers continue to express concern about the shortcomings of the unified screening mechanism (see, for example, http://www.hk-lawyer.org/content/refugee-and-non-refoulement-law-hong-kong-introduction-unified-screening-mechanism accessed December 2, 2020).

4.1.4 Japan

When implementing the Refugee Convention and 1967 Protocol into domestic law, the Japanese government revised the Immigration Control Act to create the Immigration Control and Refugee Recognition Act. This approach ensured that refugees were, and continue to be, framed as immigration problems. From 1989 to 1997, the government rejected almost all applications for refugee status. The government relied on bureaucratic rigidity (Akashi 2006) and the attitudes of immigration officers who interviewed asylum seekers to make decisions (Arakaki 2007). These officers often held that refugees must express fear and that any additional motivation (such as discriminatory treatment that prevented them from earning a living) for their departure from their former country of residence was evidence of their ineligibility for refugee status (Arakaki 2007, 296). In the early 2000s, the growth of a transnational epistemic community around refugees, the emergence of Japanese NGOs linked to that community, and the decoupling of administrative and judicial authorities that dealt with refugee recognition and appeals led to changes in the law more than twenty years after it went into force (Arakaki 2007; Dean and Nagashima 2007; Flowers 2008). Amendments to the Immigration Control and Refugee Recognition Act in 2004 included two major changes to Japan's RSD procedures. The new rule prioritized RSD procedures over deportation procedures and allowed a provisional stay so that authorities suspended deportation procedures until after immigration officials completed the RSD procedures (Akashi 2006; Flowers 2008; Dean and Nagashima 2007). The second major change was the introduction of Refugee Adjudication Counselors to consult on appeals; the goal was to improve neutrality and fairness. Nineteen counselors were appointed for two-year terms; a panel of three counselors would hear appeals of initial decisions. These counselors include experts from academia and civil society, among others. The "60-Day Rule" that required refugee recognition claims be filed within sixty days of arrival or within sixty days of the individual becoming aware of changes in the country of residence that would subject the refugee to persecution should they return was also abolished in the 2004 revision of the Act. In 2010, Japan became the first Asian country to join the group of countries with overseas resettlement programs. Japan's program is relatively small and allows for refugees from the Mae La camp on the Thai/Burma border to apply to resettle in Japan. Limiting the program to those at the Mae La camp limits Japan's resettlement to ethnic Karen.

4.1.5 South Korea

For most of the twenty years after adopting the Refugee Convention, South Korea, like Japan, framed refugees as an immigration problem. South Korea's RSD procedures were at first the same as Japan's. In 2003, the 60-day rule was changed to require a period of not more than one year, and refugees could appeal initial decisions made by a Refugee Review Committee comprised of government officials and civilians. If an appeal is rejected, an order requiring departure is issued; the applicant has ninety days to comply. During the appeal period, applicants are not allowed to work or receive assistance from the government; this can mean that government policies essentially force them to become unauthorized workers, which is grounds for deportation (Kim 2012, 228). Even after the 2003 revisions, decisions took two to three years on average. In 2008, further revisions to the Immigration Control Act aimed to improve refugees' treatment. Authorities provided legal status to those not granted refugee status but allowed to remain in South Korea on humanitarian grounds. Individuals were permitted to work during the application process, and the government acquired the authority to establish refugee support facilities (Im 2012, 588). A 2010 revision to the immigration law prioritized RSD procedures over deportation procedures, deferring deportation of those applying for refugee status or appealing a negative decision. That same year, South Korea's Ministry of Justice announced that in 2011, the RSD process would be completed within six to twelve months (Kim 2012, 226).

In December 2011, South Korea passed the first comprehensive law on refugees in East Asia. In contrast to the piecemeal revisions in the Immigration Control Act over the years, the Refugee Act is a comprehensive law that addresses refugee rights, not just the technical aspects of entering and applying for refugee status. Thus, it is a significant departure from the usual approach of immigration as a problem and the securitization of refugees; in effect, the law decouples refugee status determination from immigration law and policies. South Korea's Refugee Act defines key concepts in line with the Refugee Convention and 1967 Protocol, clearly prohibits refoulement, calls for enhancing the expertise of status determination officers, revises the functions of the Refugee Review Committee, and shortens the screening period for applications for refugee status. Importantly, the Refugee Act describes refugees' entitlements regarding social security, basic livelihood security, education, social integration programs, and the recognition of academic degrees earned abroad (Im 2012, 589). With the passage of the Refugee Act, the South Korean government also made applying for refugee status at ports of entry possible for the first time. It included a provision to allow the government to create a resettlement program, which it did in 2015.

4.1.6 Mongolia

The UNHCR Regional Bureau for Asia and the Pacific, located in Thailand, is responsible for refugee status determination decisions in Mongolia. That Mongolia's government has codified the ability of people to seek asylum in that country is a sign that the government recognizes that there are people who need to seek refuge and protection from their own government in other states. Unfortunately, the 1992 Mongolian constitution and the 2010 law reveal very narrow grounds for protection, that is, for persecution based on political beliefs. As discussed above, no policies or procedures are in place to implement these laws. Japan and South Korea allowed the UNHCR to conduct status determinations after they had become parties to the Refugee Convention but before they had instituted robust RSD procedures; the organization continues to conduct RSD in China and Hong Kong. They have offices in all four of these jurisdictions, and all except China have progressively improved their status determination over the years as they improved the capacity of their institutions, often with the help of the UNHCR. We do not know whether Mongolia will strengthen its commitment to refugee protection through institutionalizing the Refugee Convention, expanding its domestic laws to broaden the basis for asylum, establishing its own RSD procedures, and welcoming a more robust UNHCR presence in Mongolia, all of these actions or other actions that will contribute to implementing the norm of protecting refugees. Steps to become more integrated into the international system and be a reliable mediator in regional politics are hopeful signs for the future. Human rights and social welfare NGOs operate without restrictions in Mongolia. The small size of civil society organizations that are still relatively young and have yet to establish expertise or strong networks among themselves and with government actors, along with political corruption, means that they cannot yet pressure the state from below.

4.1.7 Taiwan

Taiwan has no RSD procedures, but the government has accepted asylum seekers on a case-by-case basis, which has provided inadequate protection as authorities deport some people to places where they may be at risk of persecution. As discussed earlier, cross-strait issues are central to dealing with creating a refugee policy in Taiwan. The issue is not as simple as wishing to avoid provoking Beijing. Indeed, the question of how to treat those fleeing the PRC implicates Taiwan's sovereignty. Suppose Taiwan implements a system available to all who are seeking protection. In that case, it will be obligated to treat people from the PRC, Tibet, Hong Kong, and Macau as foreigners, jeopardizing the ROC's sovereignty claim. Currently, six categories of foreigners are treated differently under Taiwan's immigration system: Chinese from the PRC, Overseas Chinese with an ROC passport, Taiwanese who have been naturalized in other countries, PRC Chinese who have been naturalized in other countries, Overseas Chinese without an ROC or PRC passport, and other foreigners (Kironska 2022). Some of those who have sought asylum in Taiwan include Tibetans, people fleeing the PRC, descendants of ROC soldiers from the conflict on the Thai-Myanmar border, people from Hong Kong, and others. Deteriorating conditions in Hong Kong have highlighted the absence of a policy in a state that relies heavily on its democratic bona fides and commitment to human rights to distinguish it from the PRC.

4.2 Conclusion

Creating policies such as those governing refugee status determination is the exclusive domain of national governments. Despite this, local activists use political space, societal support, and expertise to demand reforms when they perceive RSD procedures as inadequate or unjust. This bottom-up pressure is most effective in open societies with mature and robust civic organizations. China has no domestic RSD and no political space for organizations to form and advocate for refugee rights. Mongolia also has no domestic RSD, but it does have an active civil society that includes organizations focused on human rights. Mongolia's civil society is relatively young, and its organizations are often small, limiting their networks' organizational capacity and density. This hinders their ability to impact implementation by, for example, lobbying the government to create RSD procedures. Hong Kong has a very mature and robust civil society, as well as very strong legal institutions and a vibrant professional legal community. The advocacy of the legal community has been especially important in using the law to develop status determination procedures even though Hong Kong is not subject to the Refugee Convention, does not have RSD, and does not resettle refugees. Macau has what are formally ideal RSD procedures that fall short in practice. The nature of Macau's civil society – limited in scope with organizations that make limited demands – does not include activists who challenge the status quo and do not advocate for refugee rights. Taiwan lacks RSD procedures; the government and civil society organizations handle requests for protection on a case-by-case basis. Taiwan has a strong civil society with a high international profile, productive relations with the government, and transnational connections in the region – complicated cross-strait issues with implications for Taiwan's sovereignty limit progress on RSD. Japan and South Korea have mature, robust civil societies; their refugee advocacy organizations have strong national and transnational networks. These organizations operate in local contexts with an open society, strong legal institutions, and governments party to the Refugee Convention.

RSD procedures in East Asian countries reflect national interests, while attention to humanitarian obligations is largely absent. Framing refugee recognition as an immigration problem leads to a punitive approach that lacks transparency and confidence in refugees and their supporters. RSD procedures that attend to human rights and humanitarian obligations do so through their interview protocols and the information they gather on conditions in countries of origin. Of interest here is UNHCR's experience of training a large number of people, mostly from Southeast Asia, to do refugee status determination as part of the Comprehensive Plan of Action to address the Vietnamese refugee crisis (Bari 1992). The goal of establishing a consistent, fair, and humane system that was also attentive to differences in national interests presented a challenge. This challenge was exacerbated by most countries assigning immigration officials to undergo training to conduct interviews with those applying for refugee status. Having immigration officials conduct interviews is problematic because immigration officers have a mission that centers on securing the countries' borders, and in East Asia, in particular, securing the border is closely connected to securitizing all foreigners, including refugees. Securitizing migrants means that migrants are understood first and foremost as potential threats and treated as such. This is in contrast to an approach to refugee status determination that has the protection of refugees' human rights at the center. Most East Asian countries in this study take the same approach, as demonstrated in the tendency to situate refugee issues within immigration sections of Ministries of Justice or the equivalent. Interviewers rarely know of – let alone have expertise in – refugee law. This lack of expertise raises whether more focus on humanitarian concerns leads to better protection. The next section will consider an area of refugee protection in East Asia that seems more focused on humanitarian concerns.

5 Complementary Protection

"Complementary protection" refers to protection extended to those who do not qualify for protection under the Refugee Convention but who nevertheless are found to be in danger if returned to their country of origin. Complementary protection is based on state obligations under international law and humanitarian principles. These obligations extend to states whether or not they are party to the Refugee Convention (Foster 2009, 259–260; McAdam 2007, 48). Unlike protection under the Refugee Convention, complementary protection does not require that one be the victim of discrimination and be seeking protection based on membership in one of the protected classes enumerated in the Refugee Convention – race, religion, nationality, membership in a particular social group, or someone whose discrimination is based on political opinion. Complementary forms of protection can amplify and challenge the strengths and weaknesses of the Refugee Convention and domestic RSD procedures.

Civil society actors are often skeptical of complementary protection. Their bottom-up approach to implementation in Asia relies on a rights-based approach to refugee protection that views refugees as human rights holders (Choi 2019). Civil society actors view government reliance on complementary protection as arbitrary and opaque because they often lack clear procedures for how the status is determined. Moreover, granting complementary protection often does not include a permanent legal status, a right to work and other basic rights. They see it as a way that governments resist implementing robust refugee protection.

Officials can deny refugee status but grant the applicant permission to stay on other, usually humanitarian, grounds, or the case can be otherwise decided, such as in cases where the UNHCR might recognize refugees under its mandate and/or resettle in a third country. Japan extended complementary protection to many more people than were recognized as refugees by the government in any given year from 2008 through 2014; complementary protection was extended to at least 100 people yearly. These relatively large numbers represent a paradox of Japan's attitudes toward refugees – the government resists accepting refugees but recognizes that many need protection (Strausz 2019). Since 2014, the use of complementary protection in Japan substantially declined. The number of people receiving complementary protection in South Korea noticeably increased in 2014, the year after its comprehensive Refugee Act, which codified complementary protection, went into force.

Some nations and not others use complementary forms of protection, and their use varies in nations that use complementary protection. Where they exist, they have resulted from domestic actors leveraging other relevant international agreements, such as the Convention Against Torture, to protect refugees. In 2019, South Korea granted more applicants complementary forms of protection (222) than were granted refugee status (30), demonstrating the importance of understanding the role and impact of complementary forms of protection (see Figure 3). These can indicate that a government recognizes the need for protection while challenging international prescriptions for how they should provide that protection.

The primary argument in the literature on complementary protection is whether there is a legal basis for differential treatment of those granted protection under the Refugee Convention and beneficiaries of complementary protection. That is, does the basis upon which governments grant

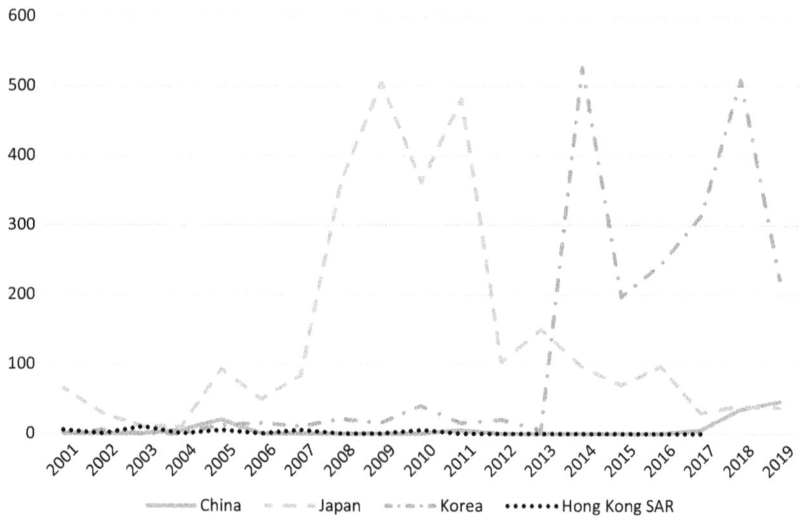

Figure 3 Complementary Protection 2001–2019.
Compiled using data from the UNHCR https://www.unhcr.org/refugee-statistics/download/?url=G6a4tv, last accessed May 7, 2021.

protection indicate a difference in the status of the protected and, therefore, a difference in the nature of protection provided? McAdam (2007) argues that there is no legal basis for differential treatment; therefore, "a legal status equivalent to that accorded by the Refugee Convention ought to apply to all persons protected by the extended principle of non-refoulement" (McAdam 2007, 1). Lister (2019) argues that there are moral grounds for distinguishing between refugees and those granted complementary protection and that this moral difference is grounds for differential legal treatment (Lister 2019, 214).

According to McAdam, the foremost expert in this area, "complementary protection" is a "form of human rights or humanitarian protection triggered by states' expanded non-refoulement obligations" (McAdam 2007, 21). The "complementary" aspect of complementary protection refers to the *source* of the additional protection. "Its chief function is to provide an alternative basis for eligibility for protection . . . .it does not mandate a lesser duration or quality of status, but simply assesses international protection needs on a wider basis than the dominant legal instrument, presently the 1951 [Refugee] Convention" (McAdam 2007, 23). The "protection" aspect of complementary protection is a "term of art in international law" as there is not a single definition or conceptualization of "protection." So, complementary protection is fluid, not fixed. Its meaning shifts depending on the meaning of "protection" under the formal refugee protection regime; "contemporary understandings of 'protection' inform its content and function" (McAdam 2007, 23). State obligations to protect refugees from being returned to places where they face danger are codified in the Refugee Convention, the Convention Against Torture (CAT), and the International Covenant on Civil and Political Rights (ICCPR). In discussions focused on refugee protection, "complementary protection" describes protection derived from a source aside from the Refugee Convention but still rooted in international human rights or humanitarian law. Some states and regions have codified complementary protection: the EU has what they refer to as "subsidiary protection," and the United States has "temporary protected status." Australia has had a complementary protection regime since 2012 (McAdam 2011). These programs provide the means to offer protection to asylum seekers who do not fit the definition of refugee under the Refugee Convention. In the United States, for example, the Secretary of Homeland Security, Alejandro Myorkas, announced a new temporary protected status designation for Haiti for eighteen months. This designation was made on May 21, 2021, and allows Haitian nationals in the United States to apply to remain in the United States due to security concerns, social unrest, increase in human rights violations, and crippling poverty that are exacerbated by the Covid-19 pandemic and the ongoing impact of the 2010 earthquake (https://www.dhs.gov/news/2021/05/22/secretary-mayorkas-designates-haiti-temporary-protected-status-18-months). In East Asia, South Korea codified complementary protection in its Refugee Act and Hong Kong has its "unified screening mechanism." I will return to this below.

The decoupling of asylum and refugee status that characterizes UN agreements traces back to the League of Nations, when the definition of refugee became a matter of international law and refugee protection through granting asylum remained an issue of state sovereignty (Gil-Bazo 2015, 2). Some argue that since the mid-twentieth century, international human rights law has become an even more important source of protection than refugee law. The scholarly debate surrounding the relative importance of each is beyond the scope of the present work. What is important is that the debate demonstrates the fluidity of the concept of complementary protection and how the issue of protection has shifted from a question of state sovereignty to one of human rights. Indeed, in allowing refugee protection to be more inclusive, international human rights law has encouraged states and the UNHCR to accept a broader category of refugees than that enumerated in the Refugee Convention and a more widespread assumption that the international community has a "*legal obligation (not merely a discretional decision)*" to protect this more inclusive category of people who may not fit the Convention definition of refugee, which requires a well-founded fear of persecution based on race, religion, nationality, political opinion, or membership in a particular social group (Gil-Bazo 2015, 1; emphasis added).

International Human Rights Monitoring Bodies (IHRMB), such as the UN Human Rights Committee, established by Article 28 of the International Covenant on Civil and Political Rights, monitor states' progress in implementing treaties domestically and their compliance with the agreements. When IHRMB evaluates country reports, this becomes an opportunity to document how committees evaluate and interpret the commitments outlined in the relevant treaties. IHRMB decisions do not establish precedent and are not necessarily legally binding; these bodies also do not make status determination decisions, but they still influence policy, legislation, implementation, and status determination insofar as their decisions find grounds for prohibition of removal after all of their domestic avenues for relief have been exhausted. IHRMBs have established an archive of decisions through which we can trace how international human rights treaties have been interpreted and how forms of complementary protection have developed.

Complementary protection has its roots in the 1960s establishment of the European Commission of Human Rights to monitor the European Convention on Human Rights and Fundamental Freedoms (ECHR). In a 1961 case against

Belgium, the Commission decided that despite the ECHR's silence on asylum and non-refoulement, the Convention does apply in cases involving forced removal. In a 1969 case against Germany, the Commission developed a formula demonstrating how removal issues can trigger states' obligations under the ECHR (Gil-Bazo 2015, 7). These findings were confirmed in a 1989 European Court of Human Rights decision against the United Kingdom. Other IHRMBs, including the United Nations Human Rights Commission, have confirmed an absolute prohibition on refoulement to places where there is a risk of torture or any of the cruel, inhuman, or degrading treatment that is mentioned in international treaties, such as the International Covenant on Civil and Political Rights, that do not explicitly provide for *nonrefoulement.* Entering into force in 1987, the Convention Against Torture is the only other international human rights treaty – aside from the Refugee Convention – that includes a specific prohibition on refoulement. Moreover, Article 3 of the Convention Against Torture is the strongest provision among the three as it does not allow exceptions or derogations: "No State Party shall expel, return ('refouler') or extradite a person to another State where there are substantial grounds for believing that he would be in danger of being subjected to torture." The clear prohibition makes the Convention Against Torture a significant source of complementary protection, including in Asia, where it has been essential in the evolution of Hong Kong's jurisprudence related to refugee protection and plays a foundational role in Hong Kong's universal screening mechanism discussed above. Concerns about international terrorism in the late twentieth and early twenty-first century greatly impacted refugee protection as states increasingly understood refugees as potential threats to state security. In its 2006 *Concluding Observations of the Human Rights Committee*, the HRC confirmed

> the *absolute nature* of the prohibition of torture, cruel, inhuman, or degrading treatment, which in no circumstances can be derogated from. Such treatments *can never be justified based on a balance* to be found between society's interest and the individual's rights under Article 7 of the Covenant. No person, without any exception, *even those suspected of presenting a danger to national security or the safety of any person, and even during a state of emergency*, may be deported to a country where he/she runs the risk of being subjected to torture or cruel, inhuman or degrading treatment.

5.1 International and Regional Agreements as Sources of Complementary Protection

Sources of complementary protection include regional and international human rights treaties, humanitarian law, humanitarian principles, and national laws.

Many countries not parties to the Refugee Convention have adopted regional agreements that address specific issues that cause people to flee. Regional agreements, such as the European Convention on Human Rights (discussed above), are important sources of complementary protection. Other regional complements to the Refugee Convention include the OAU Convention Governing the Specific Aspects of Refugee Problems in Africa, adopted in 1969 (hereafter the OAU Convention), and the Cartagena Declaration on Refugees adopted in 1984 (hereafter the Cartagena Declaration) in Latin America. These agreements were models of complementary protection when states began to take up the issue in the late 1980s (McAdam 2007, 47). In responding to regional concerns, each of these agreements expands the Convention's definition of refugees, offering protection to a broader category of people by removing persecution as a reason for fleeing and recognizing those fleeing generalized violence as refugees (Crepin 2016). In short, these agreements broaden the definition of refugee beyond the persecution of an individual based on their identity as a member of one of the protected groups enumerated in the Refugee Convention (Banerjee 2018). Notably, East Asia has no such regional agreement, but this is not surprising given that governments in East Asia tend to view refugees as economic migrants.

International human rights treaties that are complements to the Refugee Convention – including the International Covenant on Civil and Political Rights (ICCPR) and the Convention Against Torture – offer protection for those who do not fit the Convention's definition of refugee and have a significant impact on refugee policy in East Asia, especially refugee status determination. Both of these agreements oblige states to protect individuals from refoulement; this protection in these and other human rights instruments is not tied to a particular status but is accorded to all equally (Gil-Bazo 2015, 14), which is particularly important for those asylum seekers who do not fit the Convention definition of refugee. "Article 3 CAT, article 7 ICCPR and article 3 ECHR are recognized as sources of human rights non-refoulement – complementary protection – which prohibit removal in circumstances additional to (and sometimes overlapping with) article 1A(2)" of the Refugee Convention (McAdam 2007, 32). However, there is some debate about whether complementary protection is a "shield from removal" or the basis upon which migrants are allowed to enter a territory (Lister 2019, 224); this debate has significant implications for acceptance of norms of protection in East Asia.

Table 2 illustrates which international agreements codify nonrefoulement and prevent parties to the conventions – those who have signed and ratified the agreement – from returning people seeking protection to a place where they will face danger. "Yes" indicates nations that institutionalized an agreement. For UN

Table 2 Institutionalization of Refugee Convention, International Covenant on Civil and Political Rights (ICCPR), Convention Against Torture and Other Cruel, Inhuman or Degrading Treatment or Punishment (CAT) in East Asia

	Refugee Convention	ICCPR	CAT
China	Yes	Signed	Yes
Hong Kong	No	Yes	Yes
Japan	Yes	Yes	Yes
Macau	Yes	Yes	Yes
Mongolia	No	Yes	Yes
S. Korea	Yes	Yes	Yes
Taiwan	No	Yes	No

members, this is usually indicated by a state having signed and ratified an agreement. For Taiwan, institutionalization is indicated by approving and incorporating the international agreement into law. For Macau, institutionalization came when Portugal extended its obligation to the international agreement in question to its then colony, an obligation that remained when the United Kingdom transferred power over the territory to China. "No" indicates nations without action on an agreement, either by formal ratification or otherwise approving the agreement if ratification is not an option. "Signed" indicates places that have signed but not ratified the agreement and are not bound by it; China is the only nation that falls in this latter category regarding its status under the International Covenant on Civil and Political Rights.

Although (East) Asia has no regional agreement, the Bali Process facilitates state interactions on issues related to refugees and asylum seekers. The Bali Process on People Smuggling, Trafficking in Persons and Related Transnational Crime was established at the 2002 Regional Ministerial Conference on People Smuggling, Trafficking in Persons and Related Transnational Crime. It is a state-centric organization that comprises forty-five member states; seventeen observer states; three member organizations – the IOM, UNHCR, and the United Nations Office on Drugs and Crime; and thirteen observer organizations such as the Asian Development Bank, International Committee of the Red Cross and INTERPOL. The only NGO/INGO involved in the Bali Process is the International Committee of the Red Cross, and it is limited to observer status. The Bali Process is a regional consultative process that provides a forum for the Asian region to address transnational crimes around the trafficking and smuggling of goods and people. The Bali Process Ad Hoc Group was formed in 2009. It comprises nineteen members – sixteen states and three IOs – and is meant to gather the most affected member states in the region and IOs to address specific problems related to people smuggling, trafficking in persons, and irregular migration. The Regional Support Office of the Bali Process was established to facilitate cooperation on regional migration management issues, including refugee protection, human trafficking, and people smuggling. Both Japan and South Korea are members of the Bali Process, but neither are members of the Ad Hoc Group. Bali Process projects include early detection programs focused on immigration, from early detection programs focused on immigration intelligence reporting and developing the capacity of member states/immigration officers through training protection programs that offer member states a tool kit to evaluate and improve birth, marriage, and death registrations of asylum seekers, refugees and stateless persons in their territory, guidelines on identification and protection of trafficking victims, managing irregular movements by sea; migration management programs; prevention programs that include policy guidelines for criminalizing people smuggling and trafficking in persons.

Some states, including South Korea, Hong Kong, and Japan, have codified complementary forms of protection into domestic law. Theoretically, complementary protection should not differ from protection under the Refugee Convention in form or content. *Complementary* is meant to refer to the source of protection: in this case, domestic law. As McAdam explains, "It does not mandate a lesser duration or quality of status" (McAdam 2007, 23). In practice, complementary protection codified in domestic law provides asylum seekers with legal status "less comprehensive than that accorded to Convention Refugees" (McAdam 2007, 22). Complementary protection, including those codified in domestic law, is qualitatively different from the protection provided to recognized refugees.

Hong Kong, Macau, and Taiwan have complementary protection programs based on international law. Hong Kong and Macau's complementary protection policies are arguably the most robust in the region. They are "strong" insofar as they have a clear standard regarding who qualifies, standard application procedures, transparent decision-making procedures, and a stated basis in the Refugee Convention, the International Covenant on Civil and Political Rights, or the Convention Against Torture – the three agreements that explicitly enshrine protection through state obligation to observe the principle of non-refoulement.

5.2 Domestic Law as Complementary Protection

Before codifying complementary protection in domestic law, Hong Kong, Japan, and South Korea allowed some who authorities denied refugee status humanitarian permission to stay. Decision-making processes for granting this status were opaque. Although humanitarian permission to stay offered legal status, it did not include permission to work or access to social welfare benefits. When states grant humanitarian permission to stay without codified complementary protection, they elide obligation questions. This issue is not peculiar to East Asia. Until 2011, when it formally codified complementary protection in domestic law, Australia had a system that resembled what we see in much of East Asia, where, technically, refugee status determination is a separate process. However, in practice, it informs the granting of humanitarian protection. That is, granting permission to stay based on humanitarian reasons was largely seen (especially by refugee advocacy organizations) as a way to avoid granting refugee status without returning the applicants to dangerous situations. Allowing people to stay for humanitarian or compassionate reasons is based on the generosity of the state rather than a legal obligation (McAdam 2011, 60). In Australia, decisions to grant humanitarian protection often accompany denying an application for refugee status, and the basis of the decision on humanitarian status remained opaque. Prior to 1990, humanitarian status and refugee status were based on separate determination processes; an application for humanitarian protection was made based on humanitarian considerations and did not require an individual threat of discrimination, which is, of course, necessary to become a recognized refugee (McAdam 2011, 61).

Usually, states that codify complementary protection in domestic law do so intending to address a gap in protection in international or regional agreements. In the United States, for example, Temporary Protected Status is often extended to entire groups following disasters that put people at risk and force them to migrate but do not fit the Refugee Convention's definition of refugee (Frelick 2020, 43). The US government has granted nationals of Venezuela, El Salvador, and Honduras Temporary Protected Status; nationals from these countries make up most of the nearly 500,000 people in the United States who have this status. Venezuelans were first offered TPS in 2021, Salvadorans in 2001, and Hondurans in 1999. Initially, TPS is granted for six months, one year, or eighteen months, and officials can extend the protection. In September 2021, the Department of Homeland Security extended TPS for Salvadorans and Hondurans through December 2022. Venezuelans in the United States became eligible to apply for TPS in March 2021, which lasts through September 2022. Often, such attempts at creating domestic complementary protection prove ineffective for two reasons: (1) such policies often fall short of addressing the risks many asylum seekers face, and (2) the procedures for assessing each individual's asylum claim are opaque (Frelick 2020). The underlying issue is that such policies are often not based on international obligations but are viewed as demonstrations of a state's generosity. The standards are, at best, lax; at worst, they are nonexistent, applied unevenly, or applied at the discretion of the person making the decision. People granted TPS do not have a separate track to apply for citizenship or permanent residency; their status can end without much notice. There was panic when then-president Donald Trump announced the end of TPS for over 300,000 people in 2020. People with TPS from Nicaragua, Haiti, and Sudan would have seen their status end in March 2021, and those from El Salvador would have seen their status expire by November 2021. When President Joe Biden took office, he reversed this decision and extended TPS for nationals of these and two other countries through December 2022. The next section will consider which East Asian nations offer complementary protection and analyze the source of that protection: international law, humanitarian principles, or domestic statutes.

South Korea and Japan have implemented domestic statutes that protect those who fall outside the protection of the Refugee Convention. These legal frameworks are not explicitly based on international agreements and suffer from many other shortcomings that I will discuss below. China does not offer complementary protection, per se. Ethnic Kokangs, who began arriving from Burma/Myanmar in August 2009 and again in February 2015, and ethnic Kachin, who began arriving in June 2011, qualify as prima facie refugees based on the general conditions in the areas they are fleeing. They fit the Convention's definition of a religious, racial, or social group. They are allowed to stay in China as "border residents" (Song 2017, 475).

Before codifying their complementary protection policies, Japan and South Korea allowed those not granted refugee status under the law to remain for humanitarian reasons – activists often referred to it colloquially as "humanitarian permission to stay." The lack of transparency regarding who qualified for humanitarian permission to stay, the process for deciding whether they qualified, and their legal status under the program posed questions about the integrity of Japan's asylum process. In addition, like Australia's process discussed above, humanitarian permission to stay was usually granted when officials rejected an application for refugee status. Activists speculated that humanitarian permission to stay was a way for Japan to avoid its international obligations under the Refugee Convention.

Japan's Special Permission to Stay was codified in the Immigration Control and Refugee Recognition Act when it underwent major revisions in 2004 (Aycock and Hashimoto 2021). This codification was a welcome development as it legally instituted a way for the Japanese government to protect asylum seekers who did not qualify under the Convention's definition of "refugee." Despite this generally positive development, Aycock and Hashimoto's (2021) exhaustive analysis of Japan's Special Permission to Stay finds that, as written, the provision offers the government flexibility in applying the status, but the shortcomings that result from the vagueness of the language are significant. The Ministry of Justice immigration officials use their discretion to grant a Special Permission to Stay. The statute does not include clear eligibility criteria nor establish Special Permission to Stay as a right (Aycock and Hashimoto 2021, 10). A Special Permission to Stay affirms the government's discretion in offering protection in contravention of the international law understanding of refugee status as a right.

Moreover, the provision lacks the basic concept of international protection and the obligation of the Japanese state to provide such protection. The provision also does not specify the period of stay, but the visa category that it offers, designated activities, permits a one-year stay and is, in principle, renewable annually. Like other legal residents in Japan, those provided Special Permission to Stay have access to national health insurance and pension systems, but their access to social welfare benefits is questionable as the statute does not address the issue, and access to such benefits differs depending on the municipality and individual officials evaluating the application (Hashimoto 2019, 136; Aycock and Hashimoto 2021, 20). This means that some services provided for refugees are unavailable to those who receive Special Permission to Stay. Special Permission to Stay is closely tied to refugee status; receiving it depends on having applied for refugee recognition. The Immigration Control and Refugee Recognition Act "allows for the granting of [Special Permission to Stay] after authorities deny an application for refugee status, and there is no need for an applicant to request it. [Special Permission to Stay] is only granted after an application for refugee status has been denied" (Aycock and Hashimoto 2021, 21). The shortcomings of Japan's Special Permission to Stay support McAdam's assertion that domestic laws offering complementary protection provide a less comprehensive legal status than refugee recognition provides.

South Korea has also established a humanitarian status that has been refined over time. The country's 2008 revision of its Immigration Control Act included a provision to grant legal status to those not granted refugee status but are still in need of humanitarian assistance (Im 2012, 588). The 2011 Refugee Act defined key concepts, including "humanitarian status holder." Earlier drafts of the Refugee Act included more specific rights-based language, including reference to the rights of humanitarian status holders. These references were removed from the final version of the Act. The result was the continuation of a system that shares many of the shortcomings of Japan's Special Permission to Stay: unclear criteria for who qualifies, lack of access to education and social welfare programs, limited access to work permits, and short-term discretionary protection that does not offer stability or continuity of stay. Recall that Lister argued that a moral distinction between refugees and people worthy of complementary protection provides the grounds for differential legal treatment, such as differences in the duration of protection granted. This statute, with its lack of specificity in form and structure, speaks to the practical shortcomings of Lister's argument. Indeed, Japan's Special Permission to Stay and South Korea's humanitarian permission demonstrate these governments' positions that this status is based on the state's discretion, not an international obligation.

The situations in Japan and South Korea illuminate two arguments in the literature regarding complementary protection. First, the argument for a robust system of complementary protection with rights, benefits, and legal status equivalent to that provided to those recognized as refugees, and second, the argument that there is a moral basis for a different level or duration of protection for those who fall outside the parameters of the Refugee Convention. This is a significant area of investigation because authorities grant more people humanitarian permission to stay than are recognized as refugees in Japan and South Korea, countries with complementary programs based on domestic rather than international law. The fundamental issue with both of these arguments is that the humanitarian permission to stay programs in both countries fall far short of being robust complementary protection programs as defined in the literature and discussed above (Gorlick 1999; McAdam 2006; McAdam 2007; Foster 2009; McAdam 2011a; McAdam 2011b; Crepin 2016; Boom 2018; Lister 2019; Frelick 2020). How do we address this, given that there are life-and-death reasons to support various protection programs, even if they fall short of providing robust protection?

6 Conclusion

Despite the extensive rejection of the Refugee Convention in much of Asia, institutionalization in East Asia has proven to be fairly easy and widespread – five of the territories have formally institutionalized the Convention (Japan, South Korea, China, Macau, and Mongolia), and two more have institutionalized nonrefoulement (Hong Kong and Taiwan), which is central to refugee protection (see Table 3). Implementation – that is, creating laws and policies to institute refugee protection domestically – has proven far more difficult. States have more to gain from the international community through institutionalizing the Convention and are therefore more susceptible to pressure and influence from other countries when they consider adopting the Convention (Flowers 2009). The domestic political contest that ensues when governments pursue implementation seriously has far greater consequences for politics and society.

Table 3 Institutionalization and Implementation in East Asia

	Institutionalized Refugee Convention	**Refugee Status Determination Procedures**	**Complementary Protection**
China	Yes	UNHCR	No
Hong Kong	No	UNHCR	Yes
Japan	Yes	Domestic	Yes
Macau	Yes	Domestic	No
Mongolia	No	UNHCR	No
S. Korea	Yes	Domestic	Yes
Taiwan	No	None	No

In East Asia, these potential consequences include a redistribution of power in state-society relations and challenges to the widespread (but erroneous) ideology of states in the region as monoethnic societies.

While government actors have not been proactive and are even resistant to implementing the Convention, NGOs and other nonstate actors have been at the forefront of calls for implementing the Refugee Convention in East Asia. In an open society, actors have opportunities to create broad social and political support through norm diffusion, which is useful for implementation. In the cases discussed here, advocates have been central actors in diffusing refugee protection norms. Their work on norm localization, shaping international norms to cohere with domestic norms, and using their expertise translate international norms to the domestic level. These activists have led to revising existing laws as seen in Japan, the creation of new laws as in South Korea, and attempts to create laws as in Taiwan. The new comprehensive refugee law in South Korea was drafted by a national network of domestic civil society organizations working with the local office of the UNHCR and eventually negotiated with legislators. The domestic advocates leveraged their expertise in international human rights and refugee law in the process of vernacularization – making international laws intelligible at the local level. This law offers the most comprehensive refugee protection in East Asia, codifying refugees' political, economic, and social rights. We also see the global-local feedback loop between the international refugee regime and South Korea's nationally networked refugee advocacy organizations, often mediated by the Asia Pacific Refugee Rights Network. At the opposite end of the spectrum are closed societies such as China, or those with weak civil societies such as Mongolia, where there are severe limitations on the space that actors have for diffusion of refugee protection and human rights norms – there is no political space and no physical space to allow public education, networking with politicians, people at local offices of UNHCR, or other citizens – all activities that are essential for implementation.

Where there is implementation, a politically contested process unfolds over time. Whether and how governments implement refugee protection depends on civil society support and political will; each varies by context. Fewer than half of the seven jurisdictions considered here (Japan, South Korea, and Macau) have implemented refugee status determination procedures. The UNHCR conducts RSD in China, Hong Kong, and Mongolia. Refugee status determination procedures are essential because they determine refugeehood, confirm a state's decision that a person needs protection, and acknowledge responsibility to provide protection. RSD can also have political consequences since determining that people need protection makes clear that the state that they are fleeing engages in persecution. Despite the delicate nature of these decisions and the transformative impact they have on refugees, the outcomes are not based on the strength of a claim but on the design of the RSD procedures and things as arbitrary as the training or identity of the decision-maker (Costello, Nalule, and Ozkul 2020). It is possible for states that are not party to the Refugee Convention to have RSD procedures? Three jurisdictions studied here offer complementary protection, one way of providing the most basic legal protection to refugees (Japan, South Korea, and Hong Kong). South Korea and Japan have RSD and complementary protection codified into domestic law. The governments of both countries have a clear preference for granting complementary protection over refugee status. In Macau, which has established RSD procedures, we see that despite this significant step to implement the Refugee Convention, the government has not recognized any refugees since their RSD was established in 2004. Macau's weak civil society and the role that authorities in Beijing play in Macau's local politics account for this; the norm of protection has not diffused through society, and therefore, there is no demand from society for the government to fulfill its obligation and put the RSD into practice. South Korean and Japanese civil society actors are at the forefront of diffusing protection norms in the region. They use both vernacularization – whereby they act as expert translators to make international norms intelligible to domestic audiences to promote understanding, create support, and persuade governments – as well as localization – where they diffuse norms and practices learned from other activists in Asia not just norms that originate from the Western-dominated, state-centered refugee regime.

The influence that China exerts is not limited to its SARs. Indeed, China's influence ripples throughout the region. It has the largest population and economy and is the largest sender of refugees. In some cases, such as the case of Mongolia, refugees from China were deported without regard for their safety. In cases such as Japan, RSD decisions for Chinese asylum seekers were delayed for years. The region's politics and China's outsized influence in this area have implications for the implementation in each jurisdiction, especially on how all states with RSD use it. China also receives a significant number of refugees from North Korea. According to the Chinese government, North Koreans come for economic reasons and are not considered refugees. At least some of these people may need protection, but the UNHCR does not have access to this population or the region where most enter and remain. China's impact on the domestic policies of others in the region deserves much more study.

Finally, the case of China also reminds us that states and their motivations for institutionalizing international agreements can and do change over time, and this has implications for implementation. When China ratified the Refugee Convention, it sought international legitimacy as a market economy. Chinese authorities were determined to demonstrate that a democratic government was not necessary to be an engaged member of the international community and that having a democratic government was not a prerequisite for committing to human rights agreements. China's international position has since evolved to where it is now a global economic power and a serious player in East Asian and global security. This change in status impacts how China engages in international and regional politics.

Norm diffusion depends on civil society actors. These actors play a central role in diffusing norms through localization, vernacularization, and global-local feedback loops. These processes are not mutually exclusive and can occur together; one is also not more effective than the others at norm diffusion. Local context impacts which processes surface in diffusing norms locally. All three processes involve local actors diffusing norms from the global to the local level. Vernacularization relies on local actors who possess both international and local expertise, and they use their translation skills to vernacularize norms that originate in international agreements negotiated through the United Nations. This process does not challenge the Western state-centric international refugee regime with the Refugee Convention at its center. Thus, states that are more strongly tied to and engaged with the UN system are parties to the Refugee Convention, and other international human rights agreements and strong civil society organizations will see those organizations leverage the state's obligations under these agreements to push for implementation. These civil society actors will also use vernacularization to diffuse the norms domestically. Localization processes can also be used in these situations. However, they are more likely than vernacularization to be used in contexts where the state is not a party to the Refugee Convention and/or the local population is hostile to or skeptical of international norms. Localization relies on actors strongly rooted in the domestic context who can take global norms that originate from various sources, not only Western-centric sources such as the UN or international agreements. These norms can come from regional organizations such as the Asia Pacific Refugee Rights Network that help to spread practices that have worked in implementing refugee protection in one state in the region to other states. If states are not parties to international agreements, these actors do not have the option of leveraging their state's commitment to push implementation and must rely on (moral) arguments that states should implement refugee protection because it is the right thing to do based on local sense of moral obligation and doing what is right. The global-local feedback loop recognizes that diffusion is not unidirectional from the international to the domestic but that global norms are diffused locally and local norms are diffused globally in a feedback loop. The global-local feedback loop focuses on social movements as the local actors. In the case of refugee protection, we do not see social movements pressing for change, but nationally networked groups might work in concert. The regional APRRN can also work in norm diffusion in similar ways as a social movement.

NGOs, other civil society organizations, and nonstate actors, especially lawyers' groups, have taken the lead in implementing the Refugee Convention domestically in the East Asian states outside of China. As long as there is a fairly open civic culture, these groups have had space to take on significant roles in implementation. We see these actors use their roles as experts to spread the norm of refugee protection through vernacularization. The demands for change made through this process have resulted in significant reforms, including South Korea's Refugee Act – the first comprehensive refugee policy in East Asia – and Japan's refugee resettlement program. Despite these progressive moves, activists argue that governments in East Asia, including Japan and South Korea, still resist implementing the obligations of the Refugee Convention. Two examples cited to support this claim are the opacity of refugee status determination (RSD) and reliance on granting complementary protection instead of refugee status. This tendency toward humanitarian protection versus refugee status reflects the localization of protection norms; the norm of protection has been pruned, and the parts that do not cohere with local beliefs and practices – that is, broad refugee protection – have been removed. The remaining norm of humanitarian protection, which gives the authorities more control to determine who is protected, is grafted onto domestic norms to offer temporary protection to those in need. Advocates continue to work to diffuse norms and press their governments on implementation. This Element demonstrated that implementation is a contested process in all contexts, but how that contestation plays out is specific to each case.

References

Acharya, Amitav. "How Ideas Spread: Whose Norms Matter? Norm Localization and Institutional Change in Asian Regionalism." *International Organization* 58, no. 2 (2004): 239–275.

Akashi, Junichi. "Challenging Japan's Refugee Policies." *Asian and Pacific Migration Journal* 15, no. 2 (2006): 219–238.

Aleinikoff, T. Alexander. "The Unfinished Work of the Global Compact on Refugees." *International Journal of Refugee Law* 30, no. 4 (2018): 611–617.

Arakaki, Osamu. "Refugee Status in Japan: Change of Judicial Practice in the Democratic State." *Victoria University of Welington Law Review* 38, no. 2 (August 2007): 281–298.

Arakaki, Osamu, and Lili Song. "Regional Refugee Regimes." In Cathryn Costello, Michelle Foster, and Jane McAdam, eds. *The Oxford Handbook of International Refugee Law*. Oxford: Oxford University Press, 2022.

Aycock, Brian, and Naoko Hashimoto. "Complementary Protection in Japan: To What Extent Does Japan Offer Effective International Protection for Those Who Fall outside the 1951 Refugee Convention?" *Laws* 10, no. 16 (2021): 1–27.

Banerjee, Kiran. "Rethinking the Global Governance of International Protection." *Columbia Journal of Transnational Law* 56, no. 2 (2018): 313–326.

Bari, Shamsul. "Refugee Status Determination under the Comprehensive Plan of Action (CPA): A Personal Assessment." *International Journal of Refugee Law* 4, no. 4 (1992): 487–513.

Betts, Alexander, and Phil Orchard, eds. *Implementation and World Politics: How International Norms Change Practice*. Oxford: Oxford University Press, 2014.

Boom, Chirstopher D. "Beyond Persecution: A Moral Defense of Expanding Refugee Status." *International Journal of Refugee Law* 30, no. 3 (2018): 512–531

Chan, Elim, and Andreas Schloehardt. "North Korean Refugees and International Refugee Law." *International Journal of Refugee Law* 19, no. 2 (2007): 215–245.

Checkel, Jeffrey T. "International Norms and Domestic Politics: Bridging the Rationalist-Constructivist Divide." *European Journal of International Relations* 3 (1997): 473–495.

Cheng, John W., and Nicholas A. R. Fraser. "Japanese Newspaper Portrayals of Refugees – A Frame Analysis from 1985 to 2017." *Journal of Refugee Studies* 35, no. 3 (September 2022): 1364–1385.

Choi, Won Geun. "China and Its Janus-Faced Refugee Policy." *Asian and Pacific Migration Journal* 26, no. 2 (2017): 224–240.

Choi, Won Geun. "Asian Civil Society and Reconfiguration of Refugee Protection in Asia." *Human Rights Review* 20, no. 2 (2019): 161–179.

Choi, Won Geun. *Advancing Refugee Protection from Bottom-Up: Case of the Asia Pacific Refugee Rights Network (APRRN)* PhD diss, (University of Hawai'i at Manoa, 2020).

Choi, Eunyoung Christina, and Seo Yeon Park. "Threatened or Threatening?: Securitization of the Yemeni Asylum Seekers in South Korea." *Asian Journal of Peacebuilding* 8, no. 1 (2020): 5–28.

Chun, Allen. "(Post)Colonial Governance in Hong Kong and Macau: A Tale of Two Cities and Regimes." *Postcolonial Studies* 22, no. 4 (2019): 413–427.

Chung, Erin Aeran. *Immigrant Incorporation in East Asian Democracies*. Cambridge: Cambridge University Press, 2020.

Chung, Erin Aeran. "The Side Doors of Immigration: Multi-tier Migration Regimes in Japan and South Korea." *Third World Quarterly* 43, no. 7 (2021): 1–17.

Clayton, Cathryn H. *Sovereignty at the Edge: Macau and the Question of Chineseness*. Cambridge, MA: Harvard University Asia Center, 2010.

Costello, Cathryn, Caroline Nalule and Derya Ozkul. "Recognising Refugees: Understanding the Real Routes to Recognition." *Forced Migration Review* 65 (2020): 4–7.

Crawley, Heaven. "The Politics of Refugee Protection in a Post-Covid-19 World." *Social Sciences* 10, no. 3 (2021): 81.

Crepin, Mathilde. "Extended Definitions of a Refugee and Complementary Forms of Protection: An Obsolete Polarisation between Two Different Approaches to International Protection." *King's Student Law Review* 7, no. 2 (2016): 1–19.

Davies, Sara E. "The Asian Rejection?: International Refugee Law in Asia." *Australian Journal of Politics and History* 52, no. 4 (2006): 562–575.

Davies, Sara E. *Legitimising Rejection: International Refugee Law in Southeast Asia*. Leiden: Martinus Nijhoff Publishers, 2008.

Dean, Meryll, and Miki Nagashima. "Sharing the Burden: The Role of Government and NGOs in Protecting and Providing for Asylum Seekers and Refugees in Japan." *Journal of Refugee Studies* 20, no. 3 (2007): 481–508.

Fan, Chun-yip Wilson, Pui-kei Charles Fung, Yuk-fai Peter Leung, Tsz-wai Alan Tam, Cheuk-kong Vincent Wong. Administering Asylum Seekers in Hong Kong: Government Policies and Action. Unpublished Thesis. University of Hong Kong, 2016.

Flowers, Petrice R. "The International Refugee Convention: National Identity as a Limitation on Compliance." François Crépeau, ed. *Forced Migration and Global Processes: A View from Forced Migration Studies*. New York: Lexington Books, 2006, 13–34.

Flowers, Petrice R. "Failure to Protect Refugees? Domestic Institutions, International Organizations, and Civil Society in Japan." *The Journal of Japanese Studies* 34, no. 2 (2008): 333–361.

Flowers, Petrice R. *Refugees, Women, and Weapons: International Norm Adoption and Compliance in Japan*. Stanford, CA: Stanford University Press, 2009.

Flowers, Petrice R. "Crossing Borders: Transnationalism, Civil Society, and Post-9/11 Refugee Policy in Japan." David Leheny and Kay Warren, eds. *Japanese Aid and the Construction of Global Development: Inescapable Solutions*. New York: Routledge, 2010: 233–251.

Flowers, Petrice R. "International Human Rights Norms in Japan." *Human Rights Quarterly* 38 (2016): 85.

Foster, Michelle. "Non-Refoulement on the Basis of Socio-Economic Deprivation: The Scope of Complementary Protection in International Human Rights Law," *New Zealand Law Review 2009*, no. 2 (2009): 257–310.

Franck, Thomas M., and Nigel S. Rodley. "After Bangladesh: The Law of Humanitarian Intervention by Military Force." *American Journal of International Law* 67, no. 2 (1973): 275–305.

Frelick, Bill. "What's Wrong with Temporary Protected Status and How to Fix It: Exploring a Complementary Protection Regime." *Journal on Migration and Human Security* 8, no. 1 (2020): 42–53.

Gil-Bazo, Maria-Teresa. "Refugee Protection under International Human Rights Law: From *Non-Refoulement* to Residence and Citizenship." *Refugee Survey Quarterly* 34, no. 1 (2015): 11–42.

Goedde, Patricia. "Improving the Rights of Detained Asylum Seekers in South Korea." *Korea Observer* 46, no. 1 (2015): 89–115.

Goedde, Patricia. "Determining Refugee Status for North Korean Escapees under International and Domestic Laws." *Sungkyun Journal of East Asian Studies* 11, no. 2 (2011): 143–160.

Goodwin-Gill, Guy. "Forced migration: Refugees, rights and security." In Jane McAdam, ed. *Forced migration, human rights and security*. Oxford: Hart Publishing, (2008): 1–18.

Gorlick, Brian. "The Convention and the Committee against Torture: A Complementary Protection Regime for Refugees." *International Journal of Refugee Law* 11 (1999): 479–495.

Gurowitz, Amy. "Mobilizing International Norms: Domestic Actors, Immigrants, and the Japanese State." *World Politics* 51, no. 3 (1999): 413–445.

Hashimoto, Naoko. "Stratification of Rights and Entitlements among Refugees and Other Displaced Persons in Japan." Saul Takashi, ed. *Civil and Political Rights in Japan*. London: Routledge, 2019: 128–142.

Hatcher, Pascale and Aya Murakami. "The Politics of Exclusion: Embedded Racism and Japan's Pilot Refugee Resettlement Programme." *Race & Class* 62, no. 1 (2020): 60–77.

Hong, Shinae. "The Diplomatic Power of Small States: Mongolia's Mediation on the Korean Peninsula." *Australian Journal of International Affairs* 76, no. 4 (2022): 415-431.

Hung, Jason. "Why Taiwan Should Develop Exclusive Refugee Laws for Hong Kong Political Asylum Seekers so as to Defy Beijing's Interference." *Contemporary Chinese Political Economy and Strategic Relations: An International Journal* 7, no. 1 (2021): 173–185.

Hyndman, Jennifer and Johanna Reynolds. "Beyond the Global Compacts: Re-imagining Protection." *Refuge* 36, no. 1 (2020): 66–74.

Ibsen, Kailey Anne. "Refugee Law or Refugee Politics? The Varied Levels of China's Hospitality towards North Korean, Kachin, and Vietnamese Refugees." *Law School Student Scholarship Seton Hall Law* 495 (2014): 1–34.

Ieong, Meng U. and Xiangning Wu. "A Securitized 'One Country, Two Systems'? Law as Social Control in Macau." *Asian Survey* 61, no. 4 (2021): 663–682.

Im, Hyun. "An Evaluation of Korea's New Refugee Act and Future Challenges." *Korea Observer* 43, no. 4 (Winter 2012): 587–615.

Jones, Martin. "Refugee Status Determination: Three Challenges." *Forced Migration Review* 32, no. 4 (2009): 53–54.

Kalicki, Konrad. "Japan's Liberal-Democratic Paradox of Refugee Admission." *The Journal of Asian Studies* 78, no. 2 (2019): 355–378.

Kalicki, Konrad. "Fearful States: The Migration-Security Nexus in Northeast Asia." *The Pacific Review* 35, no. 1 (2022): 59–89.

Kironska, Kristina. "Taiwan's Road to an Asylum Law: Who, When, How, and Why Not Yet?" *Human Rights Review* 23, (2022): 241–264.

Kim, Hyun Mee. "'Life on Probation': Ambiguity in the Lives of Burmese Refugees in South Korea." *Asian and Pacific Migration Journal* 21, no. 2 (2012): 217–238.

Kim, Nora Hui-Jung. "Cold War Refugees: South Korea's Entry into the International Refugee Regime, 1950–1992." *Journal of Refugee Studies* 35, no. 1 (March 2022): 435–453.

Kerwin, Donald. "How Robust Refugee Protection Policies Can Strengthen Human and National Security." *Journal on Migration and Human Security* 4, no. 3 (2016): 83–140.

Kingsbury, Damien, and Leena Avonius, eds. *Human Rights in Asia: A Reassessment of the Asian Values Debate*. New York: Springer, 2008.

Klotz, Audie. *Norms in International Relations: The Struggle against Apartheid*. Ithaca: Cornell University Press, 1995.

Koizumi, Koichi. "Refugee Policy Formation in Japan: Developments and Implications." *Journal of Refugee Studies* 5, no. 2 (1992): 123–135.

Krumbein, Frédéric. "Human Rights and Democracy in Taiwan's Foreign Policy and Cross-Strait Relations." *International Journal of Taiwan Studies* 2 (2019): 292–320.

Lai, Ada Pui Yim. "Refugees and Civic Stratification: The 'Asian Rejection' Hypothesis and Its Implications for Protection Claimants in Hong Kong." *Asian and Pacific Migration Journal* 26, no. 2 (2017): 206–223.

Lee, Jieun. "A Pressing Need for the Reform of Interpreting Service in Asylum Settings: A Case Study of Asylum Appeal Hearings in South Korea." *Journal of Refugee Studies* 27, no. 1 (2014): 62–81.

Lee, Sang Kook. "The State, Ethnic Community, and Refugee Resettlement in Japan." *Journal of Asian and African Studies* 53, no. 8 (2018): 1219–1234.

Lee, Yoonkyung. "Migration, Migrants, and Contested Ethno-Nationalism in Korea." *Critical Asian Studies* 41, no. 3 (2009): 363–380.

Lie, John. *Multiethnic Japan*. Boston: Harvard University Press, 2001.

Lie, John. "The Discourse of Japaneseness." Douglass, Michael and Glenda S. Roberts, eds. *Japan and Global Migration*. London: Routledge, 2015: 69-88.

Lie, John, and Jeffrey Weng. "East Asia." In John Stone, Rutledge M. Dennis, and Xiaoshou Hou, eds. *The Wiley Blackwell Companion to Race, Ethnicity, and Nationalism*. New Jersey: Wiley-Blackewell Press 2020: 129–146.

Lister, Matthew. "Philosophical Foundations for Complementary Protection." In David Miller and Christine Straehle, eds. *The Political Philosophy of Refuge*. Cambridge: Cambridge University Press 2019: 211–230.

Loper, Kelley. "Toward Comprehensive Refugee Legislation in Hong Kong: Reflections on Reform of the Torture Screening Procedures." *Hong Kong Law Journal* 39, no. 2 (2009): 253–260.

Loper, Kelley. "Human Rights, Non-Refoulement and the Protection of Refugees in Hong Kong." *International Journal of Refugee Law* 22, no. 3 (2010): 404–439.

Lopes, Helena F. S. "The Impact of Refugees in Neutral Hong Kong and Macau, 1937–1945." *The Historical Journal* 66 (2023): 210–236.

March, James G. and Johan P. Olsen. "The Institutional Dynamics of International Political Orders." *International Organization* 52, no. 4 (1998): 943–969.

McAdam, Jane. "Seeking Asylum under the Convention on the Rights of the Child: A Case for Complementary Protection." *International Journal of Children's Rights* 14, no. 3 (2006): 251–274.

McAdam, Jane. *Complementary Protection in International Refugee Law*. Oxford: Oxford University Press, 2007.

McAdam, Jane. "From Humanitarian Discretion to Complementary Protection-Reflections on the Emergence of Human Rights-Based Refugee Protection in Australia." *Australian International Law Journal* 18 (2011): 53–76.

Mendee, Jargalsaikhan. "Renewed Geopolitical Rivalries: Challenges and Options for Mongolia." *Mongolian Geopolitics* (2022): 16–28.

Merry, Sally Engle. "Transnational Human Rights and Local Activism: Mapping the Middle." *American Anthropologist* 108, no. 1 (2006): 38–51.

Merry, Sally Engle. *Human Rights & Gender Violence: Translating International Law into Local Justice.* Chicago: University of Chicago Press, 2009.

Morico, Rachel. "Response to the Syrian Refugee Crisis in Germany, the United States, and Japan: Who Should Be Prioritized in Light of International Obligations." *Tulane Journal of International and Comparative Law* 26, no. 1 (Winter 2017): 189–210.

Morris-Suzuki, Tessa. *Borderline Japan: Foreigners and Frontier Controls in the Postwar Era.* Cambridge: Cambridge University Press, 2010.

Mukae, Ryuji. *Japan's Refugee Policy: To Be of the World.* Fucecchio, Italy: European Press, 2001.

Muntarbhorn, Vitit. *The Status of Refugees in Asia.* London: Clarendon Press, 1992.

Murphy-Shigematsu, Stephen. "Multiethnic Japan and the Monoethnic Myth." *Melus* 18, no. 4 (1993): 63–80.

Nah, Alice M. "Networks and Norm Entrepreneurship amongst Local Civil Society Actors: Advancing Refugee Protection in the Asia Pacific Region." *The International Journal of Human Rights* 20, no. 2 (2016): 223–240.

Ng, Isabella, Sharice Fungyee Choi and Alex Lihshing Chan. "Framing the Issue of Asylum Seekers and Refugees for Tougher Refugee Policy – a Study of the Media's Portrayal in Post-colonial Hong Kong." *Journal of International Migration and Integration* 2019: 593–617.

Park, Yeo Hoon Julie. "China's Way out of the North Korean Refugee Crisis: Developing a Legal Framework for the Deportation of North Korean Migrants." *Georgetown Immigration Law Journal* 25, no. 2 (Winter 2011): 515–532.

Prantl, Jochen and Ryoko, Nakano. "Global Norm Diffusion in East Asia: How China and Japan Implement the Responsibility to Protect". *International Relations* 25, no. 2 (2011): 204–223.

Price, Richard M. *The Chemical Weapons Taboo.* Ithaca, NY: Cornell University Press, 1997.

Ramsden, Michael and Luke Marsh. "The Right to Work of Refugees in Hong Kong: MA v Director of Immigration." *International Journal of Refugee Law* 25, 3 (2013): 574–596.

Reus-Smit, Christian. “Cultural Diversity and International Order.” *International Organization* 71, no. 4 (2017): 851–885, 875.

Schatte, Hans and Jennifer McCan. “The Pursuit of State Status and the Shift toward International Norms: South Korea’s Evolution as a Host Country for Refugees.” *Journal of Refugee Studies* 27, no. 3 (September 2014): 317–337.

Schloenhardt, Andreas. “Immigration and Refugee Law in the Asia Pacific Region.” *Hong Kong Law Journal* 32, no. 3 (2002): 519–548.

Siddikoglu, Hidayet. “Refugee and Asylum Seeking in Modern Japan: Analysis of Japan’s Humanitarian Commitments and Xenophobic Problems.” *The Journal of Migration Studies* 3, no. 2 (2017): 40–64.

Simeon, James C. “A Comparative Analysis of the Response of the UNHCR and Industrialized States to Rapidly Fluctuating Refugee Status and Asylum Applications: Lessons and Best Practices for RSD Systems Design and Administration.” *International Journal of Refugee Law* 22, no. 1 (2010): 72–103.

Song, Lili. “Who Shall We Help? The Refugee Definition in a Chinese Context.” *Refugee Survey Quarterly* 33, no. 1 (2014): 44-58.

Song, Lili. “Refugees or Border Residents from Myanmar? The Status of Displaced Ethnic Kachins and Kokangs in Yunnan Province, China.” *International Journal of Refugee Law* 29, no. 3 (2017): 466–487

Song, Lili. “China and the International Refugee Protection Regime: Past, Present, and Potentials.” *Refugee Survey Quarterly* 37 (2018): 139–161.

Song, Lili. *Chinese Refugee Law and Policy, 1949–2017*. Cambridge: Cambridge University Press, 2020a.

Song, Lili. “Shedding Light on RSD in China.” *Forced Migration Review* 65 (2020b): 11–13.

Strausz, Michael. *Help (Not)Wanted: Immigration Politics in Japan*. Albany: SUNY Press, 2019.

Suhrke, Astri. “The “High Politics” of Population Movements: Migration, State and Civil Society in Southeast Asia.” In Myron Weiner, ed. *International Migration and Security*. Boulder: Westview Press 1993: 179–200.

Towns, Ann E. “Norms and Social Hierarchies: Understanding International Policy Diffusion ‘From Below.’” *International Organization* 66 (2012): 179–209.

Tsutsui, Kiyoteru. “Human Rights and Minority Activism in Japan: Transformation of Movement Actorhood and Local-Global Feedback Loop.” *American Journal of Sociology* 122, no. 4 (2017): 1050–1103.

Wolman, Andrew. “Korea’s Refugee Act: A Critical Evaluation under International Law.” *Journal of East Asia and International Law* 6, no. 2 (Autumn 2013): 479–496.

Wolman, Andrew, "Japan and International Refugee Protection Norms: Explaining Non-Compliance." *Asian and Pacific Migration Journal* 24, no. 4 (2015): 409–431.

Wong, Mathew Y.H. and Ying-ho Kwong. "One Formula, Different Trajectories: China's Coalition-Building and Elite Dynamics in Hong Kong and Macau." *Critical Asian Studies* 52, no. 1 (2020): 44-66.

Yamagami, Susumu. "Determination of Refugee Status in Japan." *International Journal of Refugee Law* 7, no. 1 (1995): 60–83.

Acknowledgments

This monograph is a humble offering that I hope will be a useful comparative examination of refugee policies in East Asia. It is meant to set the table for more comprehensive comparative studies in the region. I am deeply indebted to the activists who shared their passion and expertise in refugee protection with me. I spent time with and interviewed advocates for refugee rights across Asia – in Japan, South Korea, Taiwan, and Thailand. I am deeply impressed by their energy and optimism in the face of adversity. They are advocating for some of the most marginalized people in their communities and they do so with humility. I have also had the privilege to spend time with individual refugees and refugee communities in Asia.

One refugee with whom I spent time in Thailand was curious about my experience as an African American and was surprised by how his experience as a refugee and my experience as a Black person were similar as they both raise questions of belonging and involved migration stories as central in each of our people's search for the security of belonging. We both came to where we settled as the result of forced migration – a reminder that the movement of people is not new and will continue as long as people seek security and opportunity. In fact, he seemed to have sympathy bordering on pity for my experience and this in itself made me reflect more on the constant tension between my privilege as an American abroad – a privilege that has to be constantly reasserted because I am not white – and my marginalization as a minority at home. It also reminded me that stereotypes of the Black experience travel far and wide, not unlike stereotypes of refugees.

I am fortunate to be a part of a vibrant community of scholars of Japan at the University of Hawaiʻi at Mānoa. My colleagues at the Center for Japanese Studies have been supportive of me and my research since the day I arrived on campus. I am grateful for financial support from the CJS Japan Studies Endowment, the Political Science Department, and the College of Social Sciences at UHM and for extramural funding from the Japan Society for the Promotion of Science, the Social Science Research Council, the US Fulbright Scholars Program, and the Japan-United States Education Commission. I would also like to thank the series editors and two anonymous reviewers for their careful reading of the manuscript. The final monograph is much improved because of the time and consideration of these readers. Any shortcomings that remain are due to my own limitations.

Like all projects, this one is the result of the collective energy of those who support me and my work. First and foremost is my family. One of the paradoxes of academic life for me is that I live far away from those who sustain me. What I do and what I achieve are the result of the strength that I gain from my grounding in Detroit – I often say that my family holds me down and lifts me up. Being a single parent in academia means that I must write in snatches of cobbled together time. Hopefully, my children, Isadora and Kaiya, will one day take something of value from being raised by a momma who somehow finds time for (almost) all the things and refuses to cede space that some would rather we not occupy.

This work is dedicated to my youngest brother, LaDonne. He left us too early, just as he was finding his place. Don was a great example of how to claim your space.

Cambridge Elements

Politics and Society in East Asia

Erin Aeran Chung

Johns Hopkins University

Erin Aeran Chung is the Charles D. Miller Professor of East Asian Politics in the Department of Political Science at the Johns Hopkins University. She specializes in East Asian political economy, migration and citizenship, and comparative racial politics. She is the author of *Immigration and Citizenship in Japan* (Cambridge, 2010, 2014; Japanese translation, Akashi Shoten, 2012) and *Immigrant Incorporation in East Asian Democracies* (Cambridge, 2020). Her research has been supported by grants from the Academy of Korean Studies, the Japan Foundation, the Japan Foundation Center for Global Partnership, the Social Science Research Council, and the American Council of Learned Societies.

Mary Alice Haddad

Wesleyan University

Mary Alice Haddad is the John E. Andrus Professor of Government, East Asian Studies, and Environmental Studies at Wesleyan University. Her research focuses on democracy, civil society, and environmental politics in East Asia as well as city diplomacy around the globe. A Fulbright and Harvard Academy scholar, Haddad is author of *Effective Advocacy: Lessons from East Asia's Environmentalists* (MIT, 2021), *Building Democracy in Japan* (Cambridge, 2012), and *Politics and Volunteering in Japan* (Cambridge, 2007), and co-editor of *Greening East Asia* (University of Washington, 2021), and *NIMBY Is Beautiful* (Berghahn Books, 2015). She has published in journals such as *Comparative Political Studies*, *Democratization*, *Journal of Asian Studies*, and *Nonprofit and Voluntary Sector Quarterly*, with writing for the public appearing in the *Asahi Shimbun*, the *Hartford Courant*, and the *South China Morning Post*.

Benjamin L. Read

University of California, Santa Cruz

Benjamin L. Read is a professor of Politics at the University of California, Santa Cruz. His research has focused on local politics in China and Taiwan, and he also writes about issues and techniques in comparison and field research. He is author of *Roots of the State: Neighborhood Organization and Social Networks in Beijing and Taipei* (Stanford, 2012), coauthor of *Field Research in Political Science: Practices and Principles* (Cambridge, 2015), and co-editor of *Local Organizations and Urban Governance in East and Southeast Asia: Straddling State and Society* (Routledge, 2009). His work has appeared in journals such as *Comparative Political Studies*, *Comparative Politics, the Journal of Conflict Resolution, the China Journal, the China Quarterly,* and *the Washington Quarterly,* as well as several edited books.

About the Series

The Cambridge Elements series on Politics and Society in East Asia offers original, multidisciplinary contributions on enduring and emerging issues in the dynamic region of East Asia by leading scholars in the field. Suitable for general readers and specialists alike, these short, peer-reviewed volumes examine common challenges and patterns within the region while identifying key differences between countries. The series consists of two types of contributions: (1) authoritative field surveys of established concepts and themes that offer roadmaps for further research, and (2) new research on emerging issues that challenge conventional understandings of East Asian politics and society. Whether focusing on an individual country or spanning the region, the contributions in this series connect regional trends with points of theoretical debate in the social sciences and will stimulate productive interchanges among students, researchers, and practitioners alike.

Cambridge Elements

Politics and Society in East Asia

Elements in the Series

The East Asian Covid-19 Paradox
Yves Tiberghien

State, Society, and Markets in North Korea
Andrew Yeo

The Digital Transformation and Japan's Political Economy
Ulrike Schaede, Kay Shimizu

Japan as a Global Military Power: New Capabilities, Alliance Integration, Bilateralism-Plus
Christopher W. Hughes

State and Social Protests in China
Yongshun Cai, Chih-Jou Jay Chen

The State and Capitalism in China
Margaret Pearson, Meg Rithmire, Kellee Tsai

Political Selection in China: Rethinking Foundations and Findings
Melanie Manion

Environmental Politics in East Asia
Mary Alice Haddad

Politics of the North Korean Diaspora
Sheena Chestnut Greitens

The Adaptability of the Chinese Communist Party
Martin K. Dimitrov

Refugee Policies in East Asia
Petrice R. Flowers

A full series listing is available at: www.cambridge.org/EPEA

For EU product safety concerns, contact us at Calle de José Abascal, 56–1°, 28003 Madrid, Spain or eugpsr@cambridge.org.

www.ingramcontent.com/pod-product-compliance
Ingram Content Group UK Ltd.
Pitfield, Milton Keynes, MK11 3LW, UK
UKHW020904110726
473066UK00023B/789
* 9 7 8 1 1 0 8 9 9 5 5 3 5 *